THE *Faith* OF THE PASTOR'S WIFE

Surviving in ministry yet remaining
in love with God and His people

Judith S. Hylton

WESTBOW
PRESS
A DIVISION OF THOMAS NELSON

WestBow Press books may be ordered through booksellers or by contacting:

WestBow Press
A Division of Thomas Nelson
1663 Liberty Drive
Bloomington, IN 47403
www.westbowpress.com
1-(866) 928-1240

Because of the dynamic nature of the Internet, any web addresses or links contained in this book may have changed since publication and may no longer be valid. The views expressed in this work are solely those of the author and do not necessarily reflect the views of the publisher, and the publisher hereby disclaims any responsibility for them.

Any people depicted in stock imagery provided by Thinkstock are models, and such images are being used for illustrative purposes only.
Certain stock imagery © Thinkstock.

Scripture taken from the New King James Version. Copyright 1979, 1980, 1982 by Thomas Nelson, inc. Used by permission. All rights reserved.

Scripture taken from the Holy Bible, New International Version®. Copyright © 1973, 1978, 1984 Biblica. Used by permission of Zondervan. All rights reserved.

Scripture quotations are from The Holy Bible, English Standard Version® (ESV®), copyright © 2001 by Crossway, a publishing ministry of Good News Publishers. Used by permission. All rights reserved.

ISBN: 978-1-4497-6033-5 (sc)
ISBN: 978-1-4497-6034-2 (hc)
ISBN: 978-1-4497-6032-8 (e)
Library of Congress Control Number: 2012912921

Printed in the United States of America
WestBow Press rev. date: 09/28/2012

DEDICATION

This book is dedicated to three women of faith who touched my life:
my mother Zelpha, mother-in-law Joycelyn, and Aunt Vads

CONTENTS

Part four: Transitions

Part Five: Self-care

Conclusion: Finishing well

FOREWORD

When I was a child, I spent many a Saturday afternoons watching ABC's Wild World of Sports. I was so familiar with the show that I knew what to say when Jim McKay's resonant voice said those famous lines, "The thrill of victory and the agony of defeat." In that short introduction the viewer saw an athlete celebrating in victory and in the next frame a skier falling, tumbling haphazardly over the edge of a ski jump. I always wondered what happened to the guy who failed to make the jump. Being a pastor in today's world is a lot like Wild World of Sports. The experiences are both exhilarating and at times debilitating. But what about the pastor's wife? How is the pastor's family affected during seasons of highs and lows in ministry? Eugene Peterson's book, *The Pastor: A Memoir,* explains that for his wife Jan,

> A pastor's wife was not just being married to a pastor; it was far more vocational than that, a way of life. It meant participation in an intricate web of hospitality, living at the intersection of human need and God's grace, inhabiting a community where men and women who didn't fit were welcomed, where neglected children were noticed, where the stories of Jesus were told, and people who had no stories found that they did have stories, stories that were part of the Jesus story. Being a pastor's wife would place

her strategically yet unobtrusively at a heavily trafficked intersection between heaven and earth.[1]

This is why I am thrilled to commend Judith's first book, *Faith of the Pastor's Wife*. After almost three decades of serving in ministry with me, encouraging me during some very dark days, and helping our children navigate the shifting terrain of pastoral ministry, she has finally captured not only her story, but the stories that many pastors' wives could easily tell. This book is not a lament, or an elegy about her pain and suffering. *Faith of the Pastor's Wife* celebrates faith, love for God, love for God's people and the irrepressible delight found through serving the local church. *Faith of the Pastor's Wife* is an honest retelling of how Judith Hylton has come this far by faith.

Who should read this book? Every pastor and their spouse should read this book for encouragement and the seasoned wisdom of someone who has lived in that *heavily trafficked intersection between heaven and earth*. Those entering the ministry for the first time will find principles for handling change, identity, spiritual disciplines that fortify the heart and mind toward God, and setting healthy priorities for a balanced life. Even if you are not a pastor or spouse of a pastor, members of congregations should pick up and read so as to understand your pastor and family and how best to pray for them and support them.

Congratulations on telling your story in such a winsome and accessible fashion so that millions of pastors' wives and clergy families everywhere can read this book and realize that they are not alone. May the Lord richly bless pastors and their spouses. I cannot imagine surviving in ministry without you by my side.

With gratitude and love, your husband Ray

ACKNOWLEDGEMENTS

❖ To my loving husband Ray, my best friend from age 14. You never stopped loving and supporting me in whatever venture I wanted to take on. Your life has been a testimony of unwavering faithfulness to the Lord, your family and God's people.

❖ To my children Raymond Jr., Judene and Joel: you have loved and supported your Dad and me through the ups and downs of being preacher's kids. Despite our many changes, you are still in love with God's church!

❖ To my sister Marie, sisters in law Pamela, Joy and sisters in the Lord, Donna, Karen and Grace; strong women of faith who loved me and greatly influenced my life.

❖ To all pastors' wives who shared their stories with me over the years and supported their husbands during the joys and sorrows yet never gave up.

❖ To church members in Indiana, Ohio, Pennsylvania and now Evanston, IL: Thanks for helping us raise and support our children and for offering them unconditional love.

❖ To my friends Cathy, Lynn, Barb, Carol, Lonnie and Trisha: you encouraged me when I first shared my dream of writing a book about pastors' wives.

❖ To my Lord and Savior, Jesus Christ who loved me and gave himself for me. His love and grace sustains me throughout these many years of ministry with my husband.

INTRODUCTION

Childhood dreams

CHILDHOOD DREAMS

Nobody wants to live a life that amounts to nothing. There has to be more to life than just eat, sleep, work, play, retire and then die. Ever since I was a little girl, I possessed this burning, inner desire to make my life count for something meaningful. I didn't know what that "thing" was but the desire, like a birth mark, never left me.

During my late teen years I became a Christian and my vision of living a meaningful life focused around a desire to share my life and my gifts with others and to share my testimony of Christ's love for me through music. I was not always sure how this would happen, but I knew deep inside God wanted to use me in the lives of others.

Before moving from Jamaica to America, I served the Lord as a high school teacher where I had many opportunities to interact with students. I sang in my church and also toured the island of Jamaica with a music team. Those were amazing years watching God embrace hundreds of teens and young adults into his love and mercy and listening to these young people confess Christ as Lord and Savior.

When Ray and I were married in 1983 things seemed to slow down. I moved to America and left behind my family, close friends and all my activities. I came to America in 1985 to join my husband in his first call as pastor of a small congregation in Indiana. At first I had no idea what I was getting into. I knew he was the pastor and I would pray for him and support him in every possible way. The idea of being a pastor's wife was completely outside the realm of my experience.

For almost nine years my husband faithfully served this congregation. During those early years of our marriage, I gave birth to two of our three children. By this time I was identifying myself as a wife and mother of two and still did not have any sense of identity as the pastor's wife.

I don't remember who the pastor's wife was who preceded me at this church, but after a while, people began creating expectations for me. Members of the church wanted to know if I played a musical instrument. Possibly, the former pastor's wife was a musician and therefore, I would do the same.

"Can you cook?" Someone asked me. "Are you good in the kitchen?

People were comparing me to the former pastor's wife. Was this their unspoken expectation that I would fit a similar role?

I was very upset, bewildered and pressured because I knew they hired my husband to serve the church; I was not hired to serve the congregation's preconceived expectations.

Yet despite the many spoken and unspoken expectations, those early years of ministry were some of the happiest days of my life and some of the most challenging years. I was learning how to serve alongside my husband without abdicating my sense of passion, giftedness or identity. I was learning in those early years how to glorify God and avoid being squished into the congregation's expectations of what I should be doing. I was also learning how to be a healthy family in an environment where congregations assume that the pastor's family flirts with perfection. I wanted to create a wholesome home environment for our children and our relatively young marriage. Finally, I was learning how to say no to all the urgencies that congregations foist on the pastor, his wife and his children.

PART ONE

Call

PURPOSE OF THE BOOK

This is what this book is about: after 28 years of marriage, with almost twenty-seven of those years spent serving four different congregations, I want to share some of the lessons I have learned as the wife of a pastor. Yes. I am a pastor's wife and I fully recognize that there are other ways to talk about the relationship between the pastor and spouse. Some pastors are women yet I believe that much of what I have to say still relates to female pastors and their husbands. My aim is not to enter the debate about women's ordination. My aim is to write out of my experience as a pastor's wife.

Ministry in congregations can be hard on the minister's family. This is not a gripe session. I am not a burnt-out, beat-up pastor's wife who wants to run as far as possible from the church. I love God's people and I love the local church. As Bill Hybels says, "The local church is the hope of the world,"[2] and I believe that with all my heart.

CHALLENGES OF PASTORAL VOCATION

Nonetheless, ministry is tough. The grim statistics bear this out:

- Fifteen hundred pastors leave the ministry each month due to moral failure, spiritual burnout, or contention in their churches.
- 50 percent of pastors' marriages will end in divorce.
- 80 percent of pastors feel unqualified and discouraged in their role as pastor.
- 50 percent of pastors are so discouraged that they would leave the ministry if they could, but have no other way of making a living.
- 80 percent of seminary and Bible school graduates who enter the ministry will leave the ministry within the first five years.
- 70 percent of pastors constantly fight depression.
- Almost 40 percent polled said they have had an extra-marital affair since beginning their ministry.
- 70 percent said the only time they spend studying the Word is when they are preparing their sermons.
- 80 percent of pastors' wives feel their spouses are overworked.[3]

From another angle, Dorothy Kelly Patterson shares in her *Handbook for Ministers' Wives*, rather sobering statistics:

> An informal survey conducted among pastors and their wives revealed that 63 percent of the women, compared with 44 percent of the men, believed that the pastorate is a two-person job; 78 percent of the men and 75 percent of the women agreed that the wife's active participation in church activities is necessary for the pastor to be perceived as successful. Further, 60 percent of the women and 73 percent of the men acknowledged that wives attend some activities just because they are expected to do so. However, the survey's saddest revelation is that 54.4 percent of the wives believed that their husband's first priority is the church, and 36 percent of the pastors agreed. In this framework a survey placing clergy divorces as the third highest among professional people is not too surprising. What does it mean to be a minister's First Lady? Unfortunately, the modern age has moved from "getting two for the price of one" to "settling for one for the price of two."[4]

Over many years of serving alongside my husband, I have met pastors and their wives who were so deeply discouraged and beaten up by congregational challenges that it affected the quality of their marriage, their family life and their ability to sustain their sense of call to ministry. This book aims to celebrate the joy of serving God through the local church and demonstrate how the pastor's wife might sustain love for God, her husband, her family and the family of God. Yes, it is possible with the help of the Lord to serve the local congregation and not lose your passion for people and the Lord. How does one do that? This is what I want to hopefully help you discover.

If I could re-live this part of my life, I would say especially to a new pastor's wife, make pleasing the Lord the first and most important priority in your life, then your husband. Trying to please everyone in the church is an impossible endeavor. If you are holding on to such unrealistic expectations, give it up. I learned that focusing on pleasing the Lord, not just myself, helped sustain me in my faith. This liberating way of living one's life frees one from unhealthy obsessions such as trying to make others happy, needing approval, and acceptance. If you are getting ready to serve a church then I want to talk to you. If you are already serving a church and things are hard and you feel like giving up, then you need to read what I have to say before you make a decision. If your heart is growing cold, you are suppressing your feelings of anger or hurt about something happening in your church, read my story and allow God to encourage your heart.

FULFILLMENT OF A DREAM

In 2010 I was given the opportunity to speak to a group of almost 200 women. My husband had just accepted a new call to this large church. These women came together so that I could get to know them and they could get to know me. I was asked to give my testimony and I was very excited for the chance to do this. As I got closer to the event, the Lord reminded me of some dreams I used to have. Years ago, I had dreams of speaking to groups of women. In my dreams I saw faces and places I had never seen before. Was this the fulfillment of some of my dreams? I remember sharing my visions with my husband and he would tell me, "Judith, you never know how the Lord might open doors. God has done it before and he may just do it again."

The week leading up to the event, some of the women were apologizing for not being able to attend. Finally the night of the event arrived and I was thrilled to see women streaming into the Fellowship Hall. I was also overwhelmed to see numerous women turning out to meet me. After the reception we moved to the chapel where I sang a song and then began sharing my testimony. The song that I sang, *My Soul's Desire*, was really a mini-testimony of my life. The central desire of my heart is to serve God; *to do his perfect will, to work each day and build his kingdom; this is my soul's desire.*

After the song, I stood up before this large group of women and I prayed, "Lord, this is it; use me for your glory." This would be the first time standing before so many women in what was to be my new church home. I wanted to say the right things and try to avoid making any major gaffes. I knew I had prepared what I thought was a true story of my life and God's faithfulness. Once I started speaking, all my nervousness and uncertainties melted away. I felt a deep connection with these women and began to relax and share the real me. I did not try to be funny, but the women laughed at some of the things I said. For some unforeseen reason I digressed from my notes. "Oh Judith," I said, "Keep your eyes on the script." But it only got worse. I do not know what came over me. I kept going farther and farther away from what I had planned to say. By the middle of the speech they were laughing and even some were crying.

"Well Lord, I guess they are listening," I said to myself. "Do they know that this is all real?"

"As women, we sometimes separate ourselves and avoid reaching out or allowing people to walk with us through our challenges."

"Ladies," I told them, "We need each other. This journey called life is not always easy. The Lord, who is so faithful, provides people to be his hands and feet. It would take me many hours to tell you stories of how God used people to touch my life."

"Here's what I want you to take home tonight: *Be kind to one another, tenderhearted, forgiving one another just as Christ forgave you* (Ephesians 2:32). This means God often uses others to bless us. Therefore, we should never allow our pride to prevent others from encouraging us. If we do that, we rob them from the blessing of serving the Lord on our behalf. Give people the opportunity to bless you. Allow people to minister to you."

"The second thing I want you to take home tonight is to never walk this journey alone. So if you are not part of a group of friends who can be there for you why not become part of a women's ministry, a bible study, or a small group? Get involved. You do not have to travel this journey alone. The same God whom I am talking about tonight is the same God who will carry you through. We all need each other at one time or another."

"For those of you who do not know the Lord in a personal way, now is the time to come to him; I tell you he will never fail you. He uses his people to remind us that he is there all the time and that he is a faithful God.

Thank you all for coming and remember that he who began a good work in you will be faithful to complete it."

Here I am sharing my pains, my struggles, my joys, and my sorrows with my new found friends. At the end, I challenged the women to get involved in each other's lives because deep inside this is what *I* was crying out for also. I remember speaking with intense passion about how God uses us to meet each other's needs and how I could not have made it without the love and support of people in my church and women in my life. The talk ended and the room erupted in applause. I even felt led by the Spirit to offer an altar call for those who did not know the Lord, to come to the Lord that very night.

Coming to this church was a rich blessing for us. I felt it the night I spoke to these women. I am not suggesting that every pastor's wife should be given a similar platform as I had to meet people in the church. Every person has different gifts and passions that should be used in appropriate ways. The important thing to keep in mind is that space needs to be given in every congregation for the pastor's wife to feel included and welcomed. How this happens will vary from church to church and person to person.

TRIALS STRENGTHEN NOT WEAKEN

When I was ten years old I distinctly remember telling my mother I wanted to give my heart to the Lord. Growing up and attending catholic schools, I was greatly influenced by nuns and also my Sunday school teacher, Mrs. Manning, who taught me to memorize scripture. In retrospect, they had a formative impact on my life. I even thought at one time I would like to be a nun; and I remember Sis. Anacetius, with her crisp British accent telling me, "Give yourself some time young lady, this too will pass!" She reminded the girls that we liked boys so much that chances are none of us would ever become nuns!

Over time I went through confirmation in my Anglican Church, but during those early years of my life, I drifted from the Lord and began singing secular music with a popular band in Jamaica. It was during this time that I met Ray at age fourteen. He was invited to our church by a mutual friend who was part of my youth group. His friend told him to come and check out the girls, this is how my friend Bill introduced Ray to me.

Eventually, we met each other's families and became very close friends. During this time Ray had an encounter with the Lord when he was around 17. On one occasion when he came to visit me (as he usually did and I was never home), he often spent time talking with my parents and my brothers and sister. They really liked him, especially my mother, who regularly advised me when it came to choosing boys,

"Do not look at the car look at the character." Well Ray did not have a car! He would ride his bike for many miles to see me. On one of these occasions he came to see me and I was not home but he spent considerable time talking with my brother Jimmy about the Lord. My brother told him he was too young; that when he got older he would give his heart to Christ. He wanted to first have some fun before committing his life to Christ. For some reason, Jimmy erroneously believed Christians did not know how to enjoy life.

A few weeks prior to Ray coming to visit, I had a dream that my brother had died by drowning. I told both my brothers and I vividly remember my mother saying to me after I woke up crying that it was only a dream. But it was so real.

The following Friday, after Ray spoke with him about giving his heart to the Lord, I got a call saying that my brother had died. He went fishing with a few of the boys in the neighborhood and while there, decided to go swimming with Elton, my other brother and some of his friends. His friends later told us Jimmy was trapped in a vicious undercurrent that pulled him under the water several times. Jimmy was an excellent swimmer but he was no match for this powerful under tow. Jimmy was only 15 years old when we lost him in the swirling waters of that river.

It was at my brother's funeral that I gave my heart to the Lord. On the saddest day of my life, God allowed me the grace to claim Mark 8:36 as a life scripture. It became a defining passage for how I would live the rest of my life: "What does it profit a man if he gains the whole world and loses his own soul?" The next verse asks, "What can a man give in exchange for his soul?" Of course, the answer was nothing. To God, the human soul is worth more than anything this world could ever offer. In that moment of death and sorrow, I was given a new sense of purpose and direction for my life. Instead of pursuing a career in music, I pursued serving God. At seventeen years old, instead of going to America with my band to tour and do concerts, I stayed home to help my pastor plan my brother's funeral.

I remember the devastating effect Jimmy's death had on my family. My Dad was angry at God and my mother was almost emotionally broken. She simply could not function. My sister and brothers were drowning in despair and disbelief. We honestly felt like this was a dream. We thought it wasn't real and by tomorrow we would all wake up and everything would be back to normal. But this was no dream. Life's most tragic events, if given the chance, can also result in growth, new direction and purpose for our lives. This is not always true for everyone because some people refuse to open the door and allow God to speak to them out of their personal storms. In my case, my family's tragic loss changed me. God used Jimmy's death to rewrite my life's purpose.

Today, my work as a family therapist allows me to connect at a deep level with people in various stages of pain and grief. What was a joy stealing moment in life has now become a life giving memory, allowing me to compassionately walk with people through their brokenness. It sounds like an overworked cliché, but it is true: trials do come to make us strong. Only when you have been through the fire does this make sense. God was faithful to us. And through the sustaining grace of God we were able to walk through this valley of deep shadows. I began to learn first-hand what Paul meant when he said, "God's strength is made perfect in our weaknesses (2 Corinthians 12: 9-10)." Through all our weaknesses, hardships, angry moments, and dark nights, God's strength was there to carry us along.

Some people may not understand this: but my brother's death was the seminal moment in my life and faith. This was a clarifying experience for me. This was where the turnaround came and since that day I have only focused on one objective, that is, doing all things to the glory of God instead of for my glory. I left the secular band even though some of my extended family members couldn't understand why I was making, what in their minds was a drastic decision. They thought I was over-reacting and still confused by our loss. They made it clear to me how unhappy they were with my decision to leave the group. I was on TV and singing all across the island of Jamaica and they wanted me to keep this up because it would serve to advance my nascent career. But I had no desire to do this anymore. I remembered the Lord telling me, "I will let you use your voice for my glory. You do not want earthly fame because it vanishes away so quickly."

Soon after my decision, a friend of mine, who was a pastor, asked the leader of a popular gospel group called David Keane and the Sunshine Singers to let me audition. Initially, I was not feeling excited about the audition, but I felt the nudge from the Spirit that I should go and audition. The audition went well and I was added to the group. We sang all over the Island, in schools, colleges, open air concerts, even on TV. To this day, I have vivid memories of the hundreds and thousands who came to know Christ as a result of this ministry. Even though Jimmy's death was still very fresh in my mind, I felt compelled by the Spirit to share my testimony with students, some of whom knew him or were of similar age.

Even while in college I continued singing with the group mostly on weekends. During those years, I had a front row seat to the movement and the power of the Holy Spirit over our ministry. I learned about spiritual gifts, prayer, fasting, sharing Christ, leading people to cross the line of faith and watching them commit their lives to Jesus Christ. And as God would have it, I was again on TV, but this time, singing for the Lord. The prayers of my mother were being fulfilled. She wanted me to live a radical life of service to the Lord and her prayers were being answered through means we did not and could not have anticipated.

MARRIAGE AND MOVING TO AMERICA

I n late 1980, my best friend moved to the United States of America and I thought it was good bye forever. With this big move, I assumed that God had other plans for Ray and me. But once again, my knowledge of the future was deeply flawed. About three years later, Ray came back to Jamaica and we got married in 1983 on Christmas Eve! Due to the long wait for a visa, our young marriage suffered over fourteen months of separation. But once again, our God was faithful in keeping us through those challenging times.

Nothing happens by chance. As a follower of Jesus Christ, I do not subscribe to the notion of *luck*. Jeremiah 29:11 rejects all randomness: *For I know the plans I have for you, declares the Lord, plans for welfare and not for evil, to give you a future and a hope.* The wait was so long and excruciating, some people even joked that I was lying about my marriage. "Where's your husband?" some would playfully ask. But eventually the visa, or what is called "Green Card," was granted and I was now free to travel to America and be with my husband.

I arrived in America in the heart of winter, 1985. I had never seen snow but none of this bothered me because I was joining my husband after fourteen long months of separation. Ray was already in his first year as the pastor of a church. I remember how nervous I was meeting all these new people. I was twenty four years old and a pastor's wife. In one plane ride, I went from being Judith Hylton and I was now being referred to as Pastor Hylton's wife.

But the same powerful God, who touched lives in Jamaica, was the same God who was touching people in America. This was the most grounding truth during these years of rapid change. Jesus Christ is the same, yesterday, today and forever (Hebrews 13:8).

Being new to America and new the church, I was ready to jump in and get involved in everything. But a seasoned, older woman of God kept telling me, "Sis. Judith, take it slow because the more things you are involved in, the more things folks will find to criticize you." I do not think I listened well to her counsel. Before long, I was singing, teaching Sunday school, counseling with my husband, helping with the youth group, and leading the choir. You name it, I was doing it. Back then I thought this was what the pastor's wife was supposed to do: get involved and do as much as your energy allowed you to do. In my naiveté that comes with being a twenty four year old pastor's wife, I thought all Christians loved each other. I learned my lesson very early that Christ followers are fallen people. Except for the saving mercy of God who redeems in love, the church is not possible. I am glad I learned very early that the church is a provisional community. I am under construction; the members of our congregation are also under construction. People did and said things not out of hate, but out of the gaps and need for growth in their lives. Needless to say I was going along my merry way doing what I felt was right. I was in a new church, a new country, slowly getting accustomed to the culture and even though some things were different, some things were pretty much the same. I remember the first time I went to an event at the church. I asked for a fork and this lady, with the voice of a trumpet said to me, "Honey this is called finger foods, we eat with our fingers!" I was so shocked and embarrassed but realized that she meant no harm; she was just telling me like it is. My British sensibilities needed to be tempered to my new American culture.

As a young bride I also did not understand that women would love my husband as much as I did. For example, one day a woman old enough to be my grandmother told me, "My dear if I was a little younger I would have swept that man from under your feet." That too, as naive as I was, shocked me and I think I never recovered from the sordid nature of that statement coming from a professing Christian! I still laugh even today when I think how far I have come.

Let me quickly add, this was not the norm but the exception. Most of the people I met in America were warm and accepting toward me. The party that I spoke about where the woman told me to eat with my fingers was hosted in my honor as the new pastor's wife.

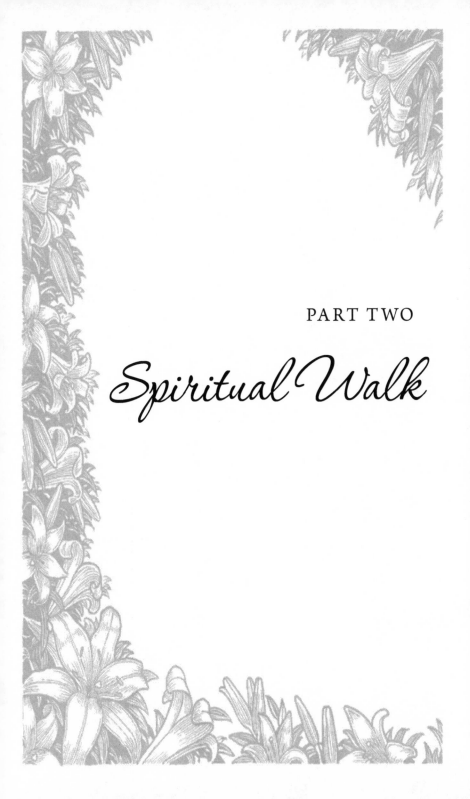

PART TWO

Spiritual Walk

PRAYER AND INTIMACY WITH GOD

Without question, prayer is the spiritual discipline sustaining my life. Daily, I bring to the Lord in prayer the many questions, challenges, and hurts of life and ministry.

There is no greater power to sustain the spiritual health of the pastor's wife than prayer. It was Corrie Ten Boom who supposedly said, "Don't pray when you feel like it. Have an appointment with the Lord and keep it. A man (or woman) is powerful on his or her knees." Why is prayer vital for your life?

First of all, Jesus modeled faithful, consistent patterns of prayer. Luke records this wonderful picture of Jesus at prayer: In these days he went out to the mountain to pray, and all night he continued in prayer to God (Luke 6:12). Prayer was the habit, the force, the source of power and spiritual connection in Jesus' life. Such must be the case for us.

But we also pray because life is fraught with battles and challenges. When our family made the decision to resign from the first church we served for almost ten years and move to North Carolina for school, we were pummeled with wave, after wave of fear and anxiety.

What if we are making the wrong move?

What if the house won't sell?

What if we move the whole family to an area that is detrimental to their well-being?

On and on the fears and doubts, like angry hornets buzzed around us. The only weapons that we could marshal to chase away our buzzing thoughts were weapons of fasting and prayer. We set aside one, sometimes two days for fasting and prayer. On one occasion we fasted for three weeks seeking God's direction for our lives. We knew that once we moved to North Carolina and the inevitable challenges came against us, we would need solid confirmation that we were in the will of God. These seasons of prayer settled us and gave us the confidence to sell our house, pack up our family and make the move to North Carolina so that my husband could continue his graduate studies.

MAKE TIME TO PRAY

Matilda Andross in her book, *Alone with God*, said these wise words,

> The great freight and passenger trains are never too busy to stop for fuel. No matter how congested the yards may be, no matter how crowded the schedules are, no matter how many things demand the attention of the trainmen, those trains always stop for fuel.[5]

Andross also encourages, "Time spent alone with God is not wasted. It changes us; it changes our surroundings; and every Christian who would live the life that counts, and who would have power for service must take time to pray."[6]

Finally, prayer is vital as the principal way to build an intimate, trust-filled relationship with Jesus Christ. "If I could hear Christ praying for me in the next room, I would not fear a million enemies. Yet distance makes no difference. He is praying for me," says Robert Murray McCheyne. This kind of intimacy often makes me feel like I am standing on an impregnable rock. So much so, that when everyone else fails, or when I fail, I rest on the sure presence of God. With this intimate walk with Christ the eyes of my understanding are open and I can see God in the little things and the big things of my life.

High on my list of prayer concerns is prayer for my children. I not only want my three children to grow up and find their place in the world, but I also want them to develop a sensitive heart for God. I pray daily that they would always make Spirit-led decisions to follow God's way rather than their own way. My husband and I are fully aware of the hollowness of trying to lead a congregation, effectively pastor God's people, and yet fail to nurture the faith of our children at home. I know that ultimately our children have minds of their own and may choose a path that we would not support. If such things were to happen, we would still love them and pray for the renewal of their hearts before God.

Because of my belief in the power of prayer and my daily exercise in these practices, I see God at work in my life, the life of the church, and the life of neighbors and friends. Each day and each week, God lays a variety of concerns on my heart. With a great sense of delight and diligence, I come into God's presence every morning and every night. The Psalmist assures me of this great truth: And those who know your name put their trust in you, for you, O LORD, have not forsaken those who seek you. (Psalm 9:10 ESV).

I remain vigilant and even militant in my prayers because of the reality of spiritual warfare. Paul was clear about the intensity of this battle:

> Finally, be strong in the Lord and in the strength of his might. Put on the whole armor of God that you may be able to stand against the schemes of the devil. For we do not wrestle against flesh and blood, but against the rulers, against the authorities, against the cosmic powers over this present darkness, against the spiritual forces of evil in the heavenly places. Therefore take up the whole armor of God, that you may be able to withstand in the

evil day, and having done all, to stand firm (Ephesians 6:10-13 ESV).

Prayer is the most potent weapon that the pastor's wife has in her arsenal to resist and withstand the powers of darkness that stand opposed to her family, the church, and her friends and loved ones. Furthermore, I know that the devil often attacks our children as a prime strategy to discourage and distract us in the work we are called to do. I pray not only for my children, but I pray earnestly for the children in our church. I pray that my children and the children of the church will love the Lord God more than anything or anyone else.

LISTEN TO HIS VOICE

Maybe you are wondering, what's the difference between praying and listening to God's voice? There is a world of difference. Prayer is not a monologue, where you the *pray-er* brings a long list of wishes and wants to God. You go through your list, say a polite amen and then launch into your day. Yes. That is prayer, but it is not the whole story on prayer. When we pray, we must also take time to listen. In this way, prayer is a dialogue; a conversation between friends, or even lovers. I speak, and then God speaks to me through prayer and His Word. What is God doing when I am praying? According to David, Evening and morning and at noon I utter my complaint and moan, and he hears my voice (Psalm 55:17 ESV). Similarly, Scripture reminds us of God's listening ability, When the righteous cry for help, the LORD hears and delivers them out of all their troubles (Psalm 34:17 ESV). So there you have it, while we are praying, our God, like the perfect host, patiently listens to us. How rude it would be after we have said what's on our heart, to simply end the conversation and walk away without waiting to hear what our heavenly host has to say? Can you imagine talking to your best friend on the phone and once you have unloaded your concerns, you hang up and end the conversation? You would not have such a friend for very long. So when we have concluded our prayers, we must now take the time to listen to God's response to us. This habit of listening to God's voice does not happen when we are distracted or in a mad rush to register our prayers. As I said, prayer is a loving conversation between two friends. So we wait, we linger and we listen for our Friend, Jesus to respond to us. We listen because God delights to communicate with his children. Almighty God is near to us through the power of the Holy Spirit.

1 O Lord, you have searched me and known me!
2 You know when I sit down and when I rise up;
you discern my thoughts from afar.
3 You search out my path and my lying down
and are acquainted with all my ways.
4 Even before a word is on my tongue,
behold, O Lord, you know it altogether.
5 You hem me in, behind and before,
and lay your hand upon me.
6 such knowledge is too wonderful for me;
it is high; I cannot attain it. Psalm 139: 1-6

I can remember occasions when the Lord impressed upon my heart that someone I knew and cared about was facing a mountain of challenges. For example, not long ago, while praying to the Lord, I received a specific burden or concern on my heart for a dear friend in another state. There was a time in my life when I ignored such impressions from the Spirit. I used to think it was just my mind. The Lord has since taught me to never ignore such words of knowledge for those He loves. I called this lady after my prayer time and she was shocked. "How did I know to call her?" Her husband had just been diagnosed with a very serious heart condition. I was not only able to pray for her, but was also able to encourage and reassure her God had heard her concerns. My calling her was a wonderful confirmation of God's promise to walk with her through this dark valley. I believe this happened because I not only prayed, but I waited for God to speak to me. Please understand, this is not some unique experience. What I am describing happens to many of God's children. Remember what James said, "Therefore, confess your sins to one another and pray for one another, that you may be healed. The prayer of a righteous person has great power as it is working. Elijah was a man with a nature like ours, and he prayed fervently that it might not rain, and for three years and six months it did not rain on the earth. Then he prayed again, and heaven gave rain, and the earth bore its fruit (James 5:16-18 ESV). Our God is awesome in power and is not a respecter of persons. I am still standing in amazement that God would choose to use an imperfect vessel like me. I know that this is all of God's grace and none of my merit. To God be all glory and praise! God desires to speak to each of his children. Our calling is to sit at his feet and listen to his voice.

As a pastor's wife, you are called to stand with the congregation and pray for your husband, their pastor. Many times I have been able to receive a word from the Lord for the church, or for my husband because I waited in God's presence for his wisdom. "The trouble with nearly everybody who prays," says Matilda Andross, "is that he says 'Amen' and runs away before God has a chance to reply. Listening to God is far more important than giving Him our ideas."[7]

The pastor's wife often hears the pain and the joys of the people in the church and what they experience. Depending on how approachable you are, people will come and talk with you about the issues they are facing. What a joy it is to know that you can touch another person's life just by being there to listen and encourage. If the pastor's wife is a woman of prayer then she will spend time interceding on behalf of the people with whom she comes into contact. The Lord says he reveals his secrets to those who love him (Psalm 25:14). If she stays faithful in prayer she will receive insight and wise words from God concerning the children of God who are hurting, grieving, happy or sad.

The pastor's wife has to be a woman of discernment. Through God's wisdom, she looks deep into the heart of her husband and knows that even though he is smiling, he is often troubled in ways that would be hidden from others. Some of these issues may concern challenges in the family, or with the church or other ministry settings. Pastors have both the awesome responsibility and the burden of shepherding God's flock. Not all the sheep follow the shepherd. Some will go astray and the pastor wants to do everything to bring lost or straying sheep back to the fold. The pastor's wife has to watch and pray; look beyond her husband's faults and see his needs. This is exactly what Jesus did even when his disciples disappointed him. He knew they were still learning how to live in obedience to his will. The pastor is human; pastors will grow weary and faint. If the pastor's wife is not prayerful in all things she can easily be ensnared in the pastor's discouragement instead of helping to lift him up out of the attitudes of self-pity and doubt.

TRUSTING GOD FOR DAILY BREAD

There were also days when our financial resources were tight. My husband would never let anyone know about our budget woes and so we had no one to talk to except the Lord. I never felt free to talk to anyone about our needs. Right or wrong, we felt the church should never know we had a need. We felt that sharing too many personal issues could unwittingly manipulate the congregation into thinking they needed to address the pastor's needs. I recognize that others may disagree with our approach, and that the church community should know about these needs out of their desire to love and support their pastor's family. Interestingly, even during our tough financial times we were still reaching out to many in their need. I remember while we were in our first pastorate the house we lived in was called the *Hylton Hotel* because we made the commitment to allow people to stay at our house.

Many years ago, after serving our very first congregation for almost 10 years, we felt God's nudge to leave. We felt clarity instead of confusion and unity within our family about the decision to resign. We sold our house, packed up our earthly possessions and left for North Carolina. While on the trip, our daughter became very ill. Fortunately, she became ill when we arrived at our destination and not while on the highway. We frantically tried to find someone to direct us to the emergency room of the local hospital. Back then we did not have a GPS or a cell phone. We drove around this unknown community for what seemed like an eternity. During our frantic search we were already tired from the long drive and now we felt as if Satan was taunting us, "What are you doing?" My husband was so strong in the midst of it. Through the power of prayer and the assistance of many kind Samaritans, we found the emergency room and got the needed medical care for her. By the next morning she was better and we were able to get the apartment we were supposed to be living in. This place sure looked better in the pictures. Nevertheless the Lord said it was the place where we were to meet the people who would touch our lives for a long time. God was so good to us; he took us through the year of uncertainty, unemployment and my husband's graduate school education. I got a job through the most miraculous means: one day a lady saw my children's bike in the front of the house and invited our children to vacation bible school. As only God can do it, this lady we met was related to a board member of a local school and this was the school I worked at for a few years while Ray was in graduate school at Duke and until we found the next call. Talk about a move of faith! Things were often precarious and tough but the Lord took care of our physical as well as our spiritual needs. It was not fun but I learned dependence on God like never before. Even my children's faith grew.

I love the passage where Jesus says, "For truly, I say to you, if you have faith like a grain of mustard seed, you will say to this mountain, 'Move from here to there,' and it will move, and nothing will be impossible for you (Matthew 17:20 ESV). I have seen God move some mighty mountains in our lives. After my husband completed his graduate work at Duke, I began praying for a job because he was now moving to a church in another state. I had given up what I thought was a great job but the Lord kept telling me to trust him for my daily needs. "Even though you have given up this job, I will bless you". Several months later I received a call from a lady I had known in North Carolina, telling me that the company she worked for was looking for someone to oversee a new expansion of this company in Ohio. If I was interested, they wanted to fly me out to the head office for an interview. This call came at a time when I was really struggling with our decision to move. With the encouragement of my husband, I accepted the job because I would be able to use my public speaking, leadership and organizational skills. After much praying and fasting I decided to take the job. This job was clearly God's gift to us. We were able to take care of our bills and continue giving to others. A sweet joy welled up in my heart when I think about the way my husband made the effort to support me in what I felt was a great opportunity to touch the lives of kids in public schools, make a great impact and be a source of encouragement to public school teachers. As Scripture says, Faith is the substance of things hoped for the evidence of things not seen (Hebrews 11: 1).

DOUBTS AND FEARS

Even though I do not have the title of Rev. so and so, I am very much a part of the thrills and agonies of pastoral ministry. I share the joys, the sorrows, the ups and downs of ministry, family and life. I often ask myself, does anyone understand what the pastor's wife feels, or what she goes through? Does anyone even care?

The saying, that the clergy family lives in a fish bowl is true. People often watch us and draw assumptions about the state of our family life. What are they saying about me, my children, and my husband? Has the picture changed over the years, or is it the same depending on which church we serve? Some days I look into the mirror before leaving for church and wonder, how will they see me, what will they say about the dress I wear, the color, the style? Maybe it is too stylish, or maybe it is too much like an old maid. Such were the questions and pressures that I faced in various stages of my life. Some members had the audacity to even question if the pastor's wife is good enough for the pastor. Furthermore, when coming into a new ministry setting, I have heard people raise the question of whether or not the pastor's wife will be similar to the former pastor and his wife.

And then there are numerous mixed and confusing signals: they want the pastor's wife to fit in and connect with the congregation and the next moment there is push back from disgruntled members who think she is too involved and is not giving members a chance to have their place in the congregation.

On the other hand, there is also pressure at home. To stay home or not to stay home, that is the question. A pastor's wife told me how she stayed home and made the care and nurture of her kids a priority. Over time the members of her congregation questioned her commitment to her husband and his ministry because she was not actively involved in the work of the church.

But when she shifted her priorities and increased her involvement in the ministry, lo and behold, someone charged, "How can she neglect her kids at home?" Can she please some and disappoint others? The pastor's wife who is she? Is she a trophy piece for all to admire by the pastor's side, or is she the thorn in some other person's side?

Sometimes my husband tries to spare me and our children from all the painful stories in the church. He does not want to burden me and he also does not want to create any sense of animosity in my children toward anyone in the church. Privately, we take all of our burdens to the Lord in prayer instead of reciting and gossiping about past hurts. The value of doing this helps us avoid nurturing a bitter, resentful, unforgiving spirit toward anyone in the congregation. God has honored our willingness to take everything to him instead of holding it in.

Of course, we also get the pleasure of hearing the joyful, uplifting stories of people being saved, marriages being healed and victories being achieved. These stories encourage us and give our family reasons to rejoice and it also confirms our call to live our lives at the center of these human events. Even though I do not preach or lead in the church as a pastor, I do feel that I am part of the ministry through my prayers and ongoing interaction and involvement with my husband and other members of the church.

Deep in my heart, I know that I am called to be supportive, have the compassion of Christ, and love for the flock my husband leads. I believe I am called to support my husband's ministry; to be by his side during times of sickness and sorrow, and even during times when the church is going through periods of conflict or is disillusioned with him. I do all I can to stand with him and affirm him.

Some who read this might think that the pastor's wife does not have an identity. This is not so. Rather, some of the pastors' wives I spoke to in preparation for this book told me that part of their calling and even their identity is to be a soul-mate with their spouse. These women are prayer giants and they know how to cry out for help to the Lord. They know the Lord to be their confidante and friend. These women know God accepts them come what may and though they are sometimes criticized and not given any acknowledgement in the way their husbands are recognized, these women find their identity in Christ's saving grace.

Some may affirm her and others may neglect to give her any credit for the many ways she quietly and with courage supports her family, her husband and the people of the church. She is there when conflicts abound; she is there during times of joy or disappointment.

But even more importantly, I have my own identity and call from God. Every woman has to know what that identity and call entails. Otherwise, she will be very unhappy and unfulfilled. This lack of clear identity in Christ is often the source of many problems in clergy families.

In my case I know that I am called to be an encourager for my husband during good times and the bad times. I am able to do this because I am knowledgeable about the most intimate challenges that he is facing every day.

Furthermore, I am called to be a woman of prayer. This is one of my spiritual gifts, the gift of prayerful intercession. I loved to stay on my knees for extended periods, crying out to the Lord my helper. I try to practice on a literal basis, Psalm 62:8: Trust in Him at all times, you people; pour out your heart before Him. God is a refuge for us (NKJV).

Despite my love for my husband, my children and the church, my first love is to the Lord. I am called to love the Lord with all my heart and strength; my husband does not come even close to the beauty and majesty of Jesus my Savior; there is no one like Jesus! Christ is my only hope and stay. He is the true source of blessing and peace every day. Therefore, when things are not going well; our children are struggling, our finances are inadequate, or even when people reject me, I have a friend, a source of comfort and solace through my relationship with Jesus Christ.

In fact this is one of the reasons why I pray that my husband's love for God would be greater than his love for me. I remain convinced that when a man loves God with all his heart, he will treat his wife like a queen. Equally, when a woman loves God with all her heart, she too will treat him as a king! So yes, I do pray that my husband's love for God would grow exponentially each day.

Another area of great fear and doubt is raising children to know and love God. What happens when your children reject Christ and turn away from the church their parents love and serve? This is an area of great pain for many families in ministry. I have sat with women and listened to their pain as they agonized over children who have gone astray.

At a recent Women of Faith conference, I sat with a pastor's wife who broke down in tears as she told me about her two children who wanted nothing to do with the church. She thinks their alienation with the church stems from the fact that the church never really nurtured or reached out to her family. Her children never had the blessing of being part of a vibrant youth group. I sat and listened to this woman unload her burden for her children. This is one of the big fears that many pastors and their wives carry. They want to make sure that after investing their lives in serving God and congregations, that something of their love for God and the church will be rooted in their children. Is there a way to encourage a growing faith in the pastor's family?

First of all, this is not a job for just the pastor's wife. The entire family has to make a commitment to follow Christ despite what is happening in the church. Faith begins at home and is often expressed and encouraged through the local church. Toward the end of Joshua's ministry he made a resolute statement about his family. The nation of Israel was getting ready to enter the land of Promise. They were faced with many problems; some were internal and some were coming from the outside. Undaunted, Joshua made the following decree before the people and his family:

> And if it is evil in your eyes to serve the LORD, choose this day whom you will serve, whether the gods your fathers served in the region beyond the River, or the gods of the Amorites in whose land you dwell. But as for me and my house, we will serve the LORD.

(Joshua 24:15 ESV). The process of nurturing the faith of the family begins with this kind of resolution, *as for me and my house*. But is this enough? Probably not.

Children have the ability to make decisions that may be contrary to the faith and values of their home. When children make such decisions, the pastor and his wife often carry significant guilt and feelings of personal failure for the spiritual state of their children's faith. I have even heard about pastors losing their jobs because their children wandered away from faith in Christ. The rationale given for firing the pastor often stems from a certain interpretation of the following instructions from Paul to Timothy regarding qualifications of an overseer:

> He (the pastor or overseer) must manage his own household well, with all dignity, keeping his children submissive, for if someone does not know how to manage his own household, how will he care for God's church (1 Timothy 3:4-5 ESV)?

Despite this teaching of Paul, it is clear one's children may go astray even when the pastor has faithfully served the Lord. Such examples are evident in the life of Noah's son (Genesis 9:24), Eli's sons, who lived contrary to their father's faith (I Samuel 2:12, 22). Even though Eli rebuked his sons and called out their sinful ways, they did not repent of their deeds. Some may wonder who was responsible for the misdeeds of these boys. God held the sons of Eli, Hophni and Phineas, responsible for their own sins because they were not only consciously sinning against others; they were consciously sinning against God. Eli was very honest with his sons about their behavior: If someone sins against a man, God will mediate for him, but if someone sins against the LORD, who can intercede for him? But they would not listen to the voice of their father (1 Samuel 2:25 ESV). This is the fear and concern many pastors' wives carry for their family.

The faith of the pastor's wife keeps her strong in the Lord and she never gives up praying for her children who have gone astray, trusting that one day they will come back to their heavenly Father who has loved them and known them before the foundations of the earth.

When the pastor's marriage or his children are facing unrest it is important that the members of the church remain understanding. This is not the time to unfairly place blame on their family. This is not the time to provide simple answers, such as, "If they were not so busy with the work of the church then their children would not have gone astray." When these troubling events happen, the pastor and his wife need the love and understanding of the church and its leaders, not their reproach or criticism.

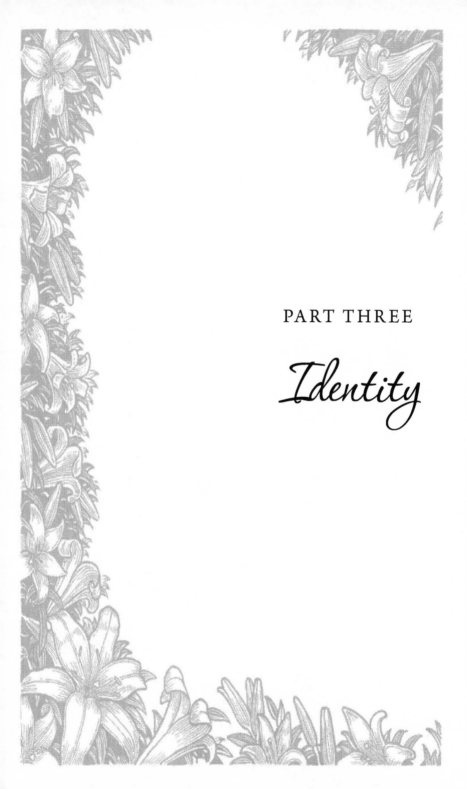

PART THREE

Identity

DISCOVERING YOUR IDENTITY

The pastor's wife, who is she?

Is she outgoing, or is she shy?

Is she warm, or cold?

Will she help with the soup kitchen, or play the piano?

Will she help with the youth or work with VBS?

Who is she?

What are her gifts and what are her talents?

The pastor's wife must know the importance of developing her own dreams and her own visions. Maybe she will only focus on her career, or maybe she will focus on her family. The camera is rolling, the stage is set, what will be the story line? Will it be a drama, a comedy, science fiction or a tragedy?

Dorothy Kelly Patterson captures well the confusion surrounding our identity:

> Too often there exists a distorted and even ridiculous image of the preacher's wife. Some view her as a brainless airhead, prey for the juiciest gossip and a sitter for the nursery. She is homely and dowdy in appearance, with out-of-date and ill-fitting clothing, a deathly countenance, no makeup, and no ornamentation. She has a sponge-like ability to absorb all criticism, graciously and without complaint, accepting martyrdom for her lifeless but pious body. She is one of the walking wounded, discouraged,

lonely, stripped of all self-worth, bereft of any friends, neglected by her husband, and unappreciated by her children. With no identity of her own, she remains in the shadow of her husband and is measured according to his success or failure. An Anglican bishop's wife once quipped, "Clergy ought to be celibate . . . because no decent, right-minded man ought to have the effrontery to ask any woman to take on such a lousy job![8]

Ideally, most people try to live their lives like an open book where the pages can be read but for some people this is not enough, they want to know more; or they have unrealistic expectations of what they think the pastor's wife should be. At times she seems intimidating to some, but too accessible for others; too outgoing for some, but too shy for others.

One of my biggest hurdles was that I often talked too much and so my prayer to the Lord was, "Lord, put a bridle on my tongue." I did not necessarily say bad things, but I did not need to tell everything. So I tried very hard when the folks at the church asked me questions to not say too much about my personal business. If I got a new dress and they admired it, I felt strange because inwardly I knew they were paying my husband a salary and at that time I did not want them to think it cost too much so I would often try to evade their inquiry by saying, "It didn't cost that much, I got it on sale". In looking back, my encouragement to pastor wives is, do not ever feel you have to give a minute by minute account of what you spend on clothes. Living under the ever watchful eyes of church members, remember—don't allow this intense scrutiny to prevent you from being yourself. My mother always said, "You are worrying about what people think about you when in fact they may be thinking about you, and then they may not be thinking about you." Don't waste your time worrying about what people think about you. Your freedom as the minister's wife comes from knowing who you are in Christ; a lesson that I am still learning after all these years. In my earlier years, I made the silly mistake of trying to get into the minds of people in the church and lived many precious days reacting to an imaginary audience: "Why did she wear this? She looks like she just walked out of Macy's catalogue," was the comment I overheard someone say to another as I walked in the building. Under pressure to fit in and avoid being a distinct individual, I sometimes changed my outfit and put on something that looked less elaborate or fussy. Thankfully, today I can say that I have become more confident and I no longer burden myself with these fears.

If I could re-live this part of my life, I would say especially to a new pastor's wife, make pleasing the Lord the first and most important thing in your life, then your husband. Trying to please everyone in the church is an impossible endeavor. If you are holding on to such unrealistic expectations, give it up. I learned that focusing on pleasing the Lord and not myself helped sustain me in my faith. This liberating way of living one's life frees one from unhealthy obsessions with being needed, approved, and accepted.

One of the realities of being a pastor's wife is the reality of being comfortable in your own skin, with your own gifts and callings. The reality is the pastor is often in the spotlight. The pastor handles much of the preaching, vision casting and leading the congregation. The pastor is highly regarded and the role of the pastor is more clearly defined in the mind of the congregation. The pastor's wife in some congregations is seen as a co-pastor and that arrangement works for those settings. But in other settings where the pastor's wife is not looked on as a leader, she is often unnoticed and even unappreciated. If this is happening to you, what should you do?

KNOW AND USE YOUR SPIRITUAL GIFTS

Remember that your pastor's wife, like any other member of the church longs to be accepted as a member of the body of Christ, endowed with her own gifts and talents. In my conversations with pastors' wives, many are confused about their role. They feel caught in the middle. They are not sure to what extent they should be involved in the ministry. But when is such involvement too much or too little? Sometimes they feel they are not supportive of their husband's ministry. What a challenging spot to be in. If you do too much you are criticized; but then you face criticism if you do too little. I tell pastors' wives just use the gifts God has given you for his glory. Do not worry about what people think. If you do you will be stressed and depressed. If you are a new pastor's wife it is best to first give yourself some time to adjust to the new ministry. Then seek God to find out where you will best fit before getting involved. You have to believe that there is a special purpose why God brought you to your current church. Remember, it is not how long you stay, but how effective you have been. Spend time in prayer and the Holy Spirit will show you how, when, where and why. Just trust him to show you your unique niche in the ministry of your church.

Paul told the church at Corinth, Now there are varieties of gifts, but the same Spirit; and there are varieties of service, but the same Lord; and there are varieties of activities, but it is the same God who empowers them all in *everyone* (even the pastor's wife). To each is given the manifestation of the Spirit for the common good (1 Corinthians 12:4-7 ESV). This means, some will have gifts of intercession, hospitality, acts of service, teaching, helps, it maybe prophecy, who knows.

As long as you keep quiet about your gifts and callings out of fear or avoidance, no one will ever know your abilities. Should you use these gifts or remain quiet? Should you focus on the gift Christ gave you or stay on the sidelines? I think the answer is clear in I Corinthians 12:7: Each person is given a manifestation of the Spirit for the common good. Therefore, congregations must make space at the table for the pastor's family to use their gifts.

If the gift is hospitality, go ahead and invite people into your home and your life for lunch, dinner, or breakfast. If you have leadership or management skills try to find ways to help plan events, serve with a committee or even serve in the community.

Some of you have wonderful gifts of helps. Your heart brims with compassion for those in need. You find joy in taking someone to the hospital, the supermarket, or even keeping someone's child while the parents are on a date. You may even have the gift of encouragement, and you enjoy sharing a timely word to lift the sagging spirit of those who are discouraged. I say, do it!

How does the pastor's wife start that new program that might encourage the advancement of the church in an area of ministry? Do it very carefully and do it mindful of the leadership and policies of the church. Never flaunt your power because you know you are the pastor's wife. The worst thing you can do is to become passive and simply sit back and watch from a distance; or aggressively advance an agenda based on the power of your relationship to your husband. I remember someone telling me how the pastor's wife before her made no contribution to the church. Of course this was false. I am sure she was making an impact where she was planted; maybe through her job or in her home. But the truth is you are always positioned by God to make an impact. I hope you get the point: knowing your spiritual gift is key to preventing over-extension of one's self. Don't venture into an area where you are not gifted. If you do not know your spiritual gift, then consider doing one of the many spiritual gift inventories found on the Internet.[9] When you know what your gift and calling is you will experience incredible freedom to be you.

Don't hesitate to say no to anything that you do not believe you are called to do. Of course there are times when you are called to make sacrifices, or even come out of your comfort zone, but even then, do so only after a period of discernment. Wait and pray and in time, the Lord will open the door for you. Humility is key.

ADAPTATION

During what some call the *honeymoon phase* of an initial call, the pastor and his wife are understandably filled with excitement. In fact, I am worried for you if you are in a new place of ministry and there is no excitement about what God wants to do. Invariably, life happens and things start to get tough. In these moments you may feel like giving up; you may even think you made a mistake and heard another voice instead of the voice of God calling you to this place of ministry.

Remember, the Lord did not say it would be easy. He promised never to leave us nor forsake us in the midst of the challenges. While Jesus was on earth he was given a mission; it was challenging and he called out to his father in heaven for strength. He never tried to do it alone so why do we fall into the trap of trying to go it alone? As the pastor's wife it is vital that you find a confidant; a shoulder to cry on and someone with whom you can be yourself; someone you can laugh and cry with; someone you can use as a sounding board.

KNOW WHO YOU ARE IN CHRIST

I would suggest that you glory in the fact that your recognition is already sealed through your relationship with Christ. The Scripture illustrates this in a dynamic way: For you have already died and your life is hidden with Christ in God (Colossians 3:3 ESV). This is the starting point for a solid identity. Our identity cannot rest on our spouse, the church, the children, or even a career, because all these things are temporary and can be taken away without warning. If your identity is forged around these external things they may quickly become idols or rivals to the heart of God.

Furthermore, a healthy congregation will embrace and affirm the unique role of the pastor's wife as separate from what the pastor does. She may have gifts in music, teaching, leadership, but she should never use these gifts out of compunction or out of a desire to prove her worth. Rather, the gifts of the pastor's wife should flow out of a recognition that she is also a member of the body of Christ and she has something to give that will edify and build the faith of the church. How sad it is when the pastor's wife is viewed as a competitor to other leaders in the church and is therefore shut out from any meaningful contribution. How sad it is when the pastor has to use the power of his office to prop up his wife's ministry or gifts. In settings like these resentment often runs high in the pastor and the congregation. All of these dysfunctional patterns are avoidable if with joy, the pastor's wife is recognized as a fellow believer in Christ who has something to offer to the church.

Discernment and prayer are required. The Lord knows the intent of your heart and he sees the motivations for your work. Trust in the Lord that he will give you that place where you can give and receive through the ministry of the church. Also, be prepared that good intentions will often be misunderstood. People may assume that you are trying to run the church, even though you have no desire to do this.

Granted, being a pastor's wife is indeed a powerful role. The power is not official, but comes through being connected with the pastor of the church. This power must be tempered with love and grace. The pastor's wife also knows many secrets about others in the church. This knowledge must be tinged with mercy and compassion. Most of all, confidentiality is required when carrying such intimate knowledge about others in the church.

When someone says, "Get a life!" there is much truth in that statement. A pastor's wife needs to have a life beyond her family, the church, and even her marriage. You are special, different, and unique. What are your dreams? What kind of career path are you considering? What do you do for fun and relaxation? Have you considered going back to school or taking a job outside the home? One of my great joys is gardening. I love to stick my fingers into the soil, plant roses, and lose myself in the beauty of God's creation. When I am outdoors gardening, or walking, my body and soul are fully alive and filled with God's contentment and peace. So ask yourself, what fills you up and brings you great joy?

Finally, another challenge facing the pastor's wife is the challenge of transparency or authenticity. I am often troubled and concerned for pastors' wives who live with extreme and conflicted emotions. For example, one view says that if the pastor's wife is unhappy she should openly express that to all. Unfortunately, this kind of raw, unfiltered, emotional expression often alienates the very people she is trying love and reach and it often confuses the members of the church. They are not sure if she is upset with her husband or the church.

On the other hand, an equally destructive emotional style says that the pastor's wife should only express happiness, laughter and contentment at all times. So even when she is hurting, tired, or downcast, her countenance must beam with the peace of God. This is just as destructive as the former emotional expression of open anger. People sometimes forget that their pastor and family are first and foremost flawed human beings. Just like other members of the church, clergy families go through times of sickness, anger, disappointment, marital strife, failure and discouragement. Thank God for healthy congregations that are mature and strong enough to grant the pastor's wife permission to be real. If she wants to entertain people, it's her call. If she wants to get involved or even sit quietly, it's her call. Give your pastor and his family the freedom to be themselves.

PART FOUR

Transitions

DEATH AND LOSS

After staying in that church for almost ten years, we moved to North Carolina. Ray went to Duke University while I taught in an Elementary school. While there, we heard the sad news that my mother was very ill. This news came at a time when I was pregnant with Joel, our third child. A week after Joel was born my Mom died. Ray, our newborn and I travelled back to Jamaica. Thankfully, Ray was able to officiate at my Mom's funeral. During this celebration of my mother's life and faithfulness to Christ and her family, my Dad, for the first time in his life accepted Christ as his Lord and Savior. This was a direct answer to prayers my mother prayed for years.

Once again, our family was faced with another challenge. Thank God that my husband, my children my church family and the Lord pulled me through those tough days. Seventeen Mother's days have come and gone and I still miss my talks with my precious mother.

The following year, Ray's dad died. In less than twenty-four months we lost another parent. Life, work, school, church, everything that allowed us to feel anchored and secure was rattled. But we were sustained by God's promises: *though I walk through dark valleys, I will fear no evil for you are with me, your rod and your staff they comfort me* (Psalm 23:4 ESV). Life brings the bitter and the sweet, good times and bad times. We were also sustained by Psalm 33:4: *for the word of the Lord is right and true he is faithful in all he does.* Our lives were violently shaken when we lost two parents in less than two years; but strangely and wonderfully, our sense of peace was intact. The hymn writer, Francis Havergal knew something of this peace:

> Stayed upon Jehovah,
> Hearts are fully blest,
> Finding, as he promised,
> Perfect peace and rest.[10]

DIRECTION

O swald Chambers says, "Never make the blunder of trying to forecast the way God is going to answer your prayers." A year ago I would have laughed like Sarah if someone told me we would move away from our home and friends in Pennsylvania to live and work in Chicago. We love Chicago but if our Jamaican blood had a hard time adjusting to the cold temperatures of Pennsylvania, we expected to have even more difficulties adjusting to some of the harsh winters in the Windy City.

Remember, never try to predict or restrain how God will lead and work in your life. I often remind myself of Solomon's wisdom: *The heart of man plans his way, but the Lord establishes his steps* (Proverbs 16:9 ESV). With both excitement and humble trust we look forward to what God will do next in this phase of our lives. As we persevere in prayer, we have seen God's hand closing some doors and opening new doors. We believe God is good and he will withhold no good thing from those who love him. God invites us to trust him. As the Scriptures say, Trust in the Lord with all your heart and lean not on your own understanding; in **all** your ways acknowledge him and he will make your paths straight (Proverbs 3: 5-6 ESV).

After being in a previous church that my husband pastored, as the new pastor's wife, I started praying about developing a women's ministry. I was eager to get this ministry up and running, but at the same time, I could not get the release in my spirit from the Lord as to when to begin. I prayed for almost two years, and then finally got the go ahead from the Lord. Remember, when God gives you the green light it does not mean there will not be any roadblocks or obstacles. I went full speed ahead and even before the first meeting, there were already many issues instigated by another person who brought a competing and divisive vision. I tried to work with the person but this was almost impossible because of the person's need to control and take power. Despite these obstacles, I moved ahead in obedience and faith and God blessed it. The women grew in their faith as a result and I also grew as I tried to include this person in all our plans. Trust the Lord for directions in all things and then your plans will succeed.

FAITHFUL FRIENDS

I have often heard the saying, "It takes a village to raise a child." While intuitively this seems true, I would also add, it takes a village to sustain a marriage and a family. Even in the midst of all that life hands us God is faithful to us in marriage. We will be married twenty nine years this Christmas Eve, 2012. The Lord entrusted to us three beautiful children Judene, Ray Jr and Joel to love and nurture as disciples of Jesus Christ. They have encountered numerous changes over the years due to our sense of God's call to the various places we felt called to serve. These changes have not always been easy for our children. They have sacrificed their comforts, familiar settings, friends, and routines for new and unfamiliar places.

Our children have always tried to openly walk with us on these adventures and in the process have grown and become more rounded. I remember when we moved to a particular area and my children were ages 14 and 16 and the youngest was getting ready for 1st grade; it was incredibly hard on them to move to another school district. My two oldest had a hard time saying goodbye to their friends. When we got to the new place they felt very isolated. They had to make all new friends. My daughter had the hardest time since she was older. The kids welcomed her at first but when it was time for *Prom* and *Home Coming* there was no one to take her. This inability to find a suitable date for the party made her very sad. I prayed earnestly to the Lord to provide a young man to take her to the Prom. God had other plans because she did attend the Prom, albeit without a date. Thankfully, the next year she did have a date. Our children openly shared with us how difficult those years were for them. We know that even though those years stretched our kids they learned lots of great life lessons.

They still have relationships with great people from prior churches and communities who loved them and greatly impacted their lives. The thing that goes unnoticed is the impact people in churches can have on the lives of our children. These influences have the potential to make or break our children. Therefore it is important that the pastor and his wife provide a *shield* around their children. Admittedly, you cannot always protect them from the words of people inside or outside the church. You cannot isolate them from the congregation. Some people may say inappropriate things about your children but of course we know our children are not perfect. When the children do or say things that are disrespectful to a church member we demand that they apologize to the adult. On the other hand, when a church member is insensitive to your children, and if you have the opportunity, approach this person in a gracious manner and help them understand some of the challenges of being a pastor's child. Encourage this person to be an extension of God's love to your children and not cut them down with unkind words.

Everyone will have an opinion about your children but you must be faithful in exposing them to people who will guide them but also correct them in love. I have been blessed as a pastor's wife by the people who have walked alongside me in the raising of my children. These were godly people who impacted my children's lives. Our children are richer because of wonderful people who were there for our family in the good times and the difficult times. Even today we still thank God for the many people in our churches who touched our lives in so many ways.

The scriptures say there is life and death in the tongue (Proverbs 18: 21). I pray that in all the places where you serve, words of life will be spoken into your children. I am convinced that we would never be able to make it as a family, a couple or even as persons without the help and support of "God's Village," the people we call the church. The greatest blessing in my life is the expressed through the Lord's faithfulness in bringing people into our lives who were willing to genuinely love us, challenge us and be reliable friends to us. As I am writing these words my mind and heart overflow with love for the countless folks who loved us and cared for us; people who stood with us when we moved to North Carolina, Ohio, Pennsylvania and now in Chicago. We felt like millionaires because of the wealth of friends given to us through the years of our ministry. When we moved to many of these places we knew no one; but by the time we moved, we had forged deep, lasting friendships with God's people. They were like angels to us and our children. Without the slightest exaggeration, I can freely say, we would not have made it without these folks coming alongside us. We had many people standing with us, helping to raise our children and loving us unconditionally. I think it is very important to receive support from your church family especially when you are in full time ministry. Not only is this a practical consideration, it is biblical to give and receive support from one another. Galatians 6:2 encourages us to, "Bear one another's burdens and so fulfill the law of Christ." Never say, "I do not need anyone to know about my needs." Of course, they are some things you may want to keep private and share only with a confidante. But it is important that you do not walk alone on this journey. Almighty God often brings people into your life to touch and change your life and so enable you to change the lives of others.

As the pastor's wife, you are also a woman of prayer. I am mentioning the importance of prayer again because prayer is like oxygen; without it our lungs collapse and survival is impossible. Pray daily for wisdom from the Lord so that what you do and say reflects compassion, tact, and consideration for others. This is important to note because the reality is after you leave the congregation and the next pastor's family comes to the church, you want to leave behind a culture, or environment that is healthy and positive toward the next pastor's family.

Your husband is an important part of your support structure but you also need other trusted women friends who listen to your joys and pains and see you for who you are. Make sure to have people in your life who love you warts and all, and do not hold a halo over your head and treat you with kid's gloves or act like you are an angel. Find people in your life who are courageous enough to speak truth into your life. We are not perfect and our position as those who stand beside our husbands does not make us incapable of doing or saying the wrong things. Just as David had a Jonathan, you need a friend or group of friends. Proverbs wisely points out, A friend loves at all time, and kinsfolk are born to share adversity (Proverbs 17:7). Solomon also says, Faithful are the wounds of a friend; profuse are the kisses of an enemy (Proverbs 27:6). Happy are those pastors' wives who have the same caliber of friends that the wisdom of Proverbs encourages.

How might you find such friends? This is a challenge I have faced as our family has served the last three churches over the last twenty-five years or more. Let's face it, when the new pastor and family arrive at the church, everyone seems friendly, caring and supportive. Young, inexperienced clergy families often open their lives very early to any and every one because of their need for belonging and fellowship. Unfortunately, I have learned the hard way that the persons who seem most attached in the early days of your coming to the church may, and I repeat, may have a hidden agenda. Therefore, one has to exercise great caution and reserve when building relationships. What has worked for me may not be applicable for your life but the following is worth considering:

1. **Pray** that God would lead you to friendships within the congregation. Pray that God would send you to people who will genuinely love you, your children, and respect the leadership of your husband. I do not share the view that it is impossible for the pastor and his family to find meaningful friendships within the church they serve. So pray for God's leading.

2. **Connect** with other pastors' wives in your area. These folks do not have to be members of your denomination. There is a somewhat universal language spoken by pastors and their spouses. This language transcends denomination, race, and even theological positions. So look around and see if there are trusted friends in the community.

3. **Start** a fellowship group for pastors' wives. When I lived on the east coast, I was saddened by the number of times I met other pastors' wives and found out just how lonely

and disconnected they were. Amazingly, there was not even a single fellowship group for pastors' wives in the area and so I decided to start one. I simply reached out and connected with one person at a time. Never once did a woman say to me she did not have interest in such a group. This confirmed to me the deep longing our sisters have for this kind of fellowship. My caution to you is that when you do meet make sure these meetings are more than a gripe session. Of course you need to give voice to your hurts and pains, but hopefully, these are times to share joys and to support each other.

Why should every pastor's wife have good and godly friends apart from the friendship of her husband? On one hand, this question seems unnecessary. I would have thought so; but after these many years, I am sorry to report the numbers of pastors and their families who live isolated lives. Just as flowers in spring need water and rain to grow, you need friends to grow. Here's why: some days are great, they are mountain top highs. But some days are lived in deep valleys where the physical and psychological demands of ministry are tiring and personally debilitating.

With the pace of ministry and the number of meetings to attend, sometimes the pastor is late getting home or comes home after the meeting and misses the opportunity to eat dinner with his family. So you find yourself eating dinner alone or alone with the children.

You need to cultivate deep friendships because some seasons of the church year are more demanding than others. For example, during fall through Christmas, the flurry of meetings, events and special services come at a dizzying pace. Fall kick-off, Thanksgiving services, Christmas parties, special services, and message preparation, committee meetings, all serve to pull your husband and you in many directions. Added to this is the pressure of the pastor's wife and her work both inside and outside the home.

As Carl Jung wrote, "Hurry is not of the devil; hurry is the devil." How do you protect yourself from this Devil called hurry and busyness? As much as possible, try to stay within bounds with your gifts, your priorities, and your energy level. Christmas is often a time when many volunteers are needed to help with pageants, parties and many special events. Don't be afraid to say no to the many invitations that will come to your inbox. If you do say yes, be prepared to face praises from some and criticisms from others.

Some of the more spiritually minded might say, "I have a friend in Jesus and need no other." This kind of thinking misses the point. Even Jesus, who had an incredibly intimate relation with the Father, had close friendship with his disciples and an even closer relationship with three men, Peter, James and John. So I would say you need both: foster a close walk with Christ *and* with people in your community. May God give you great wisdom as you pursue building a support structure.

LEAVING A CHURCH,
OR THE CHURCH ASKS YOU TO LEAVE

There comes a time in ministry when the pastor and family sense the need to move; there also comes a time when some churches demand that the pastor moves. I remember getting a call from a pastor's wife asking for prayer for her husband as he was planning to leave the church they had served for several years. I can still remember the anguish, fear and anger in her voice. She wanted to stay at the current church but her husband wanted to leave. Thankfully, she knew how to pray and even though it was a challenge, she supported her husband and they made the move. For the pastor's wife, decisions like this come frequently for those serving in itinerant contexts, such as Methodists, or hierarchical settings where the bishop has influence in determining where the pastor serves.

Either way, moving by choice or forced termination, a pastoral move is hard on the family. Depending on the age of your children, the extent to which you and your children are embedded in key relationships in the church and community, moving to another church and community can have long term effects on the family. My oldest child still talks about a move we made back in the early nineties. More than a decade later, my adult child still talks about the pain and loneliness our decision to move caused her.

When our family moved, I felt like I had to be a doctor to my children and husband; patching bruises, applying loving support and counsel to everyone was my call. Depending on the age of the children, my husband and I had to spend considerable time explaining why we needed to move.

Innocently they asked, "Why are we moving mom? Did daddy do something wrong?"

"Oh no," I replied over and over, trying to soothe their troubled hearts. "The Lord is moving us on." Even when I said that, I knew I was raising more questions than answers for them. This is what I have faced each time we moved. Thankfully, we have not moved many times.

Once the decision to move is made, what assurance do you have that it will work? I have learned in these moments of uncertainty to trust the Lord to take us through the transitions.

Our most recent move is an example of trusting God through each stage. Because our youngest son had to finish school, I remained in the community while my husband moved on to the new church. This time of separation was hard for me and our son. Looking back, I know that it was the support of my friends outside the church that helped us through the period of separation. Unfortunately, this is an awkward time for the members of the former church. Where do you go to church after your husband moves but you are still in the community? I could not go back to the church because the new pastor and his family were now in place. It was hard for the church because they needed to support their new clergy family and yet they wanted to reach out to me. I finally decided to discontinue my attendance at the church and this gave us the chance to visit other congregations that we were never able to experience because of being in our own church those many years. Having friends outside the church was truly my main lifeline. These women were not part of our former congregation and therefore felt no conflict of interest.

On most days, I felt like I was standing before a huge mountain of decisions; other days I felt I was in a valley teeming with fears about the future. My mind tried to process a barrage of questions:

- Will my children develop good friends?
- Will I find healthy connections with the people of this new church?
- Will I connect with new neighbors where we live?
- Will my husband's ministry flourish?

All these questions bombarded my mind. What could I do but call out to my Lord Jesus, and heavenly Father to help me stay positive, and to trust in God to meet all our needs. Every move to a new church stretched our faith. We struggled to find a house and struggled to sell our house in our former community. There were some low days when I began doubting, "Did God really open this door?" If he did, why are things so hard?

The greatest lesson we have learned that helped with any decision to move was the lesson of prayer. We never moved from a church because it was difficult, or because we received a call to a bigger church or a higher salary. Never make a move based on trivial pursuits. Make sure when a move is being contemplated that God is in the details; that God has placed it on your heart and is giving you several confirmations. If you are not seeing God's hand confirming your plans then stay put.

Furthermore, we never made a move unless we were of one mind about the move. This principle has undoubtedly saved us from many disasters. There were times when my husband was excited about a possible move and I could not shake the sense that this was the wrong time or wrong place. Instead of claiming his right or authority, my husband respected my sense of God's leading and waited. We have never been disappointed by choosing to wait on God.

A great example of waiting on God comes from the life of Moses' leadership in the wilderness:

On the day that the tabernacle was set up, the cloud covered the tabernacle, the tent of the testimony. And at evening it was over the tabernacle like the appearance of fire until morning. So it was always: the cloud covered it by day and the appearance of fire by night. And whenever the cloud lifted from over the tent, after that the people of Israel set out, and in the place where the cloud settled down, there the people of Israel camped. At the command of the LORD the people of Israel set out, and at the command of the LORD they camped. As long as the cloud rested over the tabernacle, they remained in camp. Even when the cloud continued over the tabernacle many days, the people of Israel kept the charge of the LORD and did not set out. Sometimes the cloud was a few days over the tabernacle, and according to the command of the LORD they remained in camp; then according to the command of the LORD they set out. And sometimes the cloud remained from evening until morning. And when the cloud lifted in the morning, they set out, or if it continued for a day and a night, when the cloud lifted they set out. Whether it was two days, or a month, or a longer time that the cloud continued over the tabernacle abiding there, the people of Israel remained in camp and did not set out, but when it lifted they set out. At the command of the LORD they camped, and at the command of the LORD they set out. They kept the charge of the LORD, at the command of the LORD by Moses (Numbers 9:15-23).

Someone wisely said, "Time spent waiting on God is never wasted." If the cloud does not move, stay put!

Being a pastor's wife involves dealing with many challenges. Not just the challenge of location but also vocation. The move affects not only the pastor and children, but when the pastor moves or goes to another church it also means the pastor's wife may have to change her career. If the *cloud* is not moving it could mean that God wants you to stay where you are, or he wants you to be patient and trust him. It is very important that you and your spouse are on the same page; otherwise, it will be very hard to discern God's voice.

We have had several examples when we witnessed God's hand in our tough decisions. I remember when we were deciding to make a move to a particular city. We sought the Lord as much as we could because we were quite comfortable where we were and never thought we would move. Periods of fasting and praying became the order of the day. We spent many hours wrestling with the Lord for a whole year. We started getting confirmations that assured us that the Lord was leading us to this new ministry. As we sought the Lord he confirmed it first to my husband and then he confirmed it to me. Some of you are asking, "How did we know? We got the answer through a process of prayer, time in God's word, and through the prayerful support of friends who counseled us and prayed for us. When we shared our plans with our dear friends they helped us discern God's plan; God spoke to us through their wisdom.

I remember when my husband had a strong desire to go back to school and do additional graduate work. For some reason though, he kept questioning whether or not he could do it. I kept encouraging him, reminding him that God would use his added training and education in every aspect of his life and work. Finally he agreed with me, applied to the school and was accepted.

On another occasion he felt in his heart that the Lord wanted him to move to another church. We only had been there for 4 years as the associate pastor. We fasted and prayed, and through the counsel of many trusted advisers, felt it was the right time to move. This was hard for our church and the senior pastor to accept, but they were very gracious and allowed us to leave with their blessing. To this day we stay in touch with many of the families of this church. If you are going to leave make sure that the ending is as healthy as possible for the people and your family. "Don't burn your bridges," as the saying goes.

Sometimes when unfortunate events transpire in a church, we tend to forget the good times—and we had many good times—such as congregations that blessed our family with surprise birthday parties; significant gifts to our family that enabled us to take trips to Jamaica; fixing our roof when it was leaking, babysitting our children, mentoring our children, giving wise advice and most of all, for loving us even though we did not always get it right. Don't ever allow the bad times to cloud the memories of kindness shown. Put yourself in their shoes: it is important to remember that the church loves your family; they may have invested years in your life, loving you, connecting with you and building strong bonds of trust. When you announce your plans to leave it will not be easy to see their pastor and family walk through the door. The greatest feeling though is when you have said your goodbyes, trusting in the Lord to send another pastor to shepherd the flock, and it happens! There is no greater joy to later hear that your former congregation now has a new pastor they love and respect and together are dreaming big kingdom goals. It is almost as if they are getting an added confirmation that you correctly discerned God's plan for your life and for the congregation's life.

Without question, the hardest part of leaving a church is helping to process the hurt and anger of those who feel abandoned by your leaving. This is a delicate time for me. This is also a delicate time for children, youth and families of the church. Great care must be taken how the message is communicated to staff and families of the church. Remember, if the cloud or the fire does not move, stay where you are and trust God. God's way is always better and wiser than your way!

PART FIVE

Self-care

THE IMPORTANCE OF SELF-CARE

Ministry is tough. The mental, emotional and physical demands are extensive. Clergy families who fail to take vacations, days off, study leave, meaningful rest and relaxation are asking for trouble. Some pastors are so busy they ignore warning signs and keep pushing on; running dangerously on empty. After all, how admirable it appears to see your pastor expending upwards of 60 hours or more per week at the church without a single day off! If this is your story, for the sake of your marriage, the care of your children and the health of the pastor and congregation, get off the treadmill.

With the voice of first-hand experience, Wayne Cordiero warns, "We don't forget that we are Christians. We forget that we are human, and that one oversight alone can debilitate the potential of our future."[11]

This is the same advice Jethro gave to Moses when he visited him in the wilderness. "When Moses' father-in-law saw all that he was doing for the people, he said, "What is this that you are doing for the people? Why do you sit alone, and all the people stand around you from morning till evening?" And Moses said to his father-in-law, "Because the people come to me to inquire of God; when they have a dispute, they come to me and I decide between one person and another, and I make them know the statutes of God and his laws." Moses' father-in-law said to him, "*What you are doing is not good.* You and the people with you will certainly wear yourselves out, for the thing is too heavy for you. You are not able to do it alone (Exodus 18:14-18 ESV)."

What you are doing is not good! Unfortunately, Wayne Cordiero says we believe the lie that while this happens to other weak pastors, it could never happen to us:

> One of the common anesthetics that numb us to these dark harbingers is thinking, "It could never happen to me!" The signs were all around me, but I ignored them. Simple problems refused solution. Anything that necessitated emotional energy sent me in the other direction. My faith was bruised and fragile. My confident demeanor had turned pensive, and a soul that used to be an ocean of life was now a stagnant tide pool.[12]

Every pastor and spouse should tape this quote several places in their home to remind them to slow down. Jettison your messiah complex, your distorted thinking that you are going to die trying to save the church or the world. Intentionally plan and schedule time away. This is hard for me to do. I sometimes set up plans for a night out, or a week away, and then something happens at the church, a person dies, or a conflict erupts and our plans have to change. We still go ahead and set a date but we try to be flexible, knowing that things may change without advance notice.

Find a mentor or a more experienced clergy family and try to discover what they do to sustain their marriage, their emotional and physical health. Remember, ministry in the church is not a sprint; it is more like a marathon. Experienced runners know how to pace themselves and not expend all their energy in the first mile.

I have heard of clergy families going on vacations with members of their churches. If you feel a real connection with folks in your church go ahead and take that time away. Just make sure this is a time of refreshment, relaxation and prayer designed to build up your family. Don't take the cares of the church with you on these trips. We have made the mistake of going on planned vacations but we returned more drained and depleted because we spent some of our vacation with friends, family who had many needs for prayer and counseling. We have even made the mistake of preaching at other churches while on vacation! I know, this is crazy and we made many silly mistakes during our early years. Time away for rest, relaxation and a change of pace is critical to sustaining meaningful relationship with your spouse and children, but also just to rest. There are at least 12 examples of Jesus in Luke withdrawing to desolate places to pray (Luke 5: 16). If Jesus had to take time away, what about us? Make it a habit of withdrawing for a few days to regroup as a family and evaluate where you are in your relationship with God and your leadership of the church.

NURTURING YOUR MARRIAGE

Related to self-care is the care of your marriage. Our philosophy is to do the best we can to set our priorities in the right order. What do I mean by this? In order to nurture a healthy marriage as a couple, God has to be first priority in your life. My husband often agreed with me that if his love for God is paramount, then his treatment of me will be healthy and God-honoring.

The second priority is love for your family. We often say, "What good is it to gain the whole church, grow the church, reach many people for Christ and then lose your family?" I have often heard this analogy: the shoemaker makes shoes for all the families in the village and yet his children have shoes with holes or have no shoes. Our greatest accomplishment in ministry would be to see our children walking with the Lord and giving their lives to him in total submission. We would have failed to a certain degree if our church family thinks we are the best and yet our children think we are irresponsible and neglectful of their needs. In my time as a pastor's wife I have met many unhappy clergy spouses who wear a plastic smile before the congregation but in private conversations, reveal deep anger and resentment that the church has more value than the needs of the family. So the first priority is God; the second is your family.

The third priority is your vocation or your call to ministry. One's ministry in the church is important but it should never come before love for God and love for one's family. Ministry in the church becomes a joyful experience when the other priorities are in place. Furthermore, the members of the congregation will respect you when they see you display a healthy balance between family and church.

Having balanced priorities go a long way to protect your marriage. In unhealthy situations where one's priorities are skewed, the pastor is often unable to ward off unhealthy relationships, corrosive stress, and the tendency to engage in poor decision making. Stressed out pastors often bring their stress into the home and the impact on their marriage and their children is sad and devastating.

Over the years, my husband and I have recognized these pitfalls and while we have not completely mastered these challenges, we have worked hard to mitigate them by taking certain commonsense precautions.

We would encourage every clergy couple to attend Dennis Rainey's, *A Weekend to Remember* marriage conference.[13] We attended these retreats several times because we felt this event encouraged us in our marriage, but on our limited budget we were grateful that they offered the retreat free of charge to clergy couples.[14] Even if you think your relationship is rock solid, as one person said, *the biggest room in the world is the room for improvement.* If the idea of *A Weekend to Remember* marriage seminar is not your forte, then choose to attend a marriage retreat that speaks to you and your spouse. The important thing is to do something.

We also made it a regular part of our life together to go out on a date night. From the earliest days of our marriage my husband and I have taken Fridays as a day off from the church and spent it together doing a variety of things. Even when we had our three children at home, we found a responsible baby sitter and went out on a date. Our feeling then and now was that our marriage would fall apart without proper maintenance and care.

I want to share a prayer from the book, *The power of a praying wife* by Stormie Omartian. May this prayer help you as you seek to establish Spirit driven priorities:

> *God, I proclaim you Lord over my life. Help me to see you first every day and set my priorities in perfect order. Reveal to me how to properly put my husband before children, work, family, friends, activities and interests. Show me what I can do right now to demonstrate to him that he has this position in my heart. Mend the times I have caused him to doubt that. Tell me how to prioritize everything so that whatever steals life away or has no lasting purpose will not occupy my time. I pray for my husband's priorities to be in perfect order as well. Be Lord and Ruler over his heart. Help him to choose a simplicity of life that will allow him to have time alone with You, Lord, a place to be quiet in your presence every day. Speak to him about making Your Word, prayer and praise a priority. Enable him to place me and our children in greater prominence in his heart than career, friends, and activities. I pray he will seek you first and submit his will to You, for when he does, I know the other pieces of his life will fit together perfectly.*[15]

Of course, I would say a hearty, amen to this prayer!

SECOND PAIR OF EYES

While doing premarital counseling with my former pastor he told me that I was to be my husband's second pair of eyes. He recounted a personal story of how a woman in his congregation was trying to make inappropriate inroads into his life. His wife was very sensitive to the woman's overtures and alerted him. He openly shared with me that his wife's actions kept him from falling into a trap that the devil had set for him. This is a very sensitive area. The pastor's wife is caught in an interesting dilemma as she observes her husband's interactions with women in the congregation. I have learned over the years that my task is not to keep women away from my husband; my mission is to pray for him in all areas of his life. I pray for covering over his mind and protection over his body. I pray that no weapon that is fashioned against him shall succeed (Isaiah 54:17). I pray that any trap the enemy has set for him will fail. The Psalmist says, but let all who take refuge in you rejoice;

> let them ever sing for joy,
> and spread your *protection* over them,
> that those who love your name may exult in you.
> For you bless the righteous, O LORD;
> you cover him with favor as with a shield.
> (Psalm 5:11-12 ESV)

If the pastor deliberately, or carelessly moves from under God's covering or protection, or from listening or trusting when his wife warns him about the need to exercise caution, there is little she can do physically to restrain or prevent such things from happening. But all is not lost. Seek the support of friends and trusted counselors and remain vigilant in prayer. This battle is not yours, it is the Lord's. When the disciples of Jesus asked him to teach them to pray, he told them to also say, And lead us not into temptation, but deliver us from evil (Matthew 16:13). The point is we are all susceptible to a variety of temptations. This is one of the important points found in *The power of a praying wife*:

> Temptation is everywhere today and we are fools if we or our husbands can't be lured by it in some form other. The bible says, the eyes of man are never satisfied (Proverbs 27:20). If that's true, temptation is always a possibility and we must be ever watchful . . . . The enemy of our souls knows where our flesh is weakest and he will put temptation in our paths at our most vulnerable points.[16]

Almost daily we hear horrible stories of pastors having affairs or of priests in the Catholic Church molesting children, or of pastors in trouble with the law for stealing and the question one asks is, why? Is it because this man just chooses to behave this way? When a pastor falls into sexual sin, such failures cause irreparable damage and shame to the church, the family, the community, and most of all, such failure dishonors the name of Christ. Stanley Grenz, in *Betrayal of Trust*, depicts the damage of clergy misconduct in stark terms:

> "It is a violation of a sacred sexual trust, marring the beautiful picture God has given of the relationship of Christ and the church. And it is a violation of a power trust, abusing the privilege of the pastoral position with

which the ordained leader has been endowed by the church and its Lord."[17]

Some pastors' wives are afraid to say what they feel lest they are perceived as being jealous. I have a few cases where I felt uncomfortable because of how a woman responded to my husband. I have come to realize over the years that some of these women were not even aware that they were acting inappropriately. Sometimes, because the pastor is warm and friendly some women think it is an opening to get a bit closer.

In *Betrayal of Trust*, a book every pastor and family should read, Stanley Grenz reminds the reader of one of the most famous cases of clergy sexual misconduct in American history and the extent to which people conspired to protect the pastor:

> In 1868 Henry Ward Beecher (1813-1887), the renowned pastor of Plymouth Congregational Church in Brooklyn Heights, New York, began visiting Elizabeth Tilton, a congregant and the wife of a close friend. He hoped to console her on the death of her child. Their relationship continued, however, until several years later rumors of impropriety led Elizabeth Tilton's husband to lay charges against the pastor. Despite overwhelming evidence of their pastor's guilt, Plymouth Church stood by him. In 1878 the congregation excommunicated those who had testified against Beecher, including Elizabeth Tilton. She died in 1897, ostracized and alone.[18]

I have a friend of mine who was in ministry who warned her husband about a woman but the husband ignored it. Unfortunately, the woman's husband did have an affair, but through the grace of God and the intervention of many caring people, they were able to save their marriage. Satan's mission is to destroy pastors and their wives so he can destroy the effectiveness of their ministry. My advice is to pray covering over your family each day. Pray that your marriage would be nurtured in a healthy, God-honoring way.

The pastor often receives lots of affirmation from people in the church but if this affirmation is not taking place at home, this could be an easy trap the enemy uses to gain a foothold. Over the years I have had women say things to me about my husband. I remember one woman brashly telling me that I am naive to think I am the only woman attracted to my husband. I was shocked and hurt by her words. I have since forgiven this woman but I am sure she has no idea how deeply her words disturbed me. The pastor has to also make sure that his wife feels secure and not put other people in the church before her. Their relationship needs to be guarded and protected. Unfortunately, if the marriage is shaky it is the easiest way to open the door in ways that undermine the health of the marriage. Continue to affirm your husband as Gary Chapman advices in his book, *The Five love languages*, we must be willing to learn our spouse's primary love language if we are to be effective communicators of love.[19]

If the pastor's love language is affirmation and every time he is at the church, or elsewhere someone else keeps affirming him and you are not doing it, this could be a problem. The day you shared your marriage vows, you both made a covenant for life and for keeps. You made a covenant to love honor and cherish.

People often say to me, "how do you do it? You keep a clean house and your children are so all well-behaved." I usually tell them I do the same thing every wife and mother would do, which is, love your family unconditionally, set the atmosphere for the home, cover your home in prayer and trust in the Lord to build the home (Psalm 127:1).

Regarding prayer, I again encourage you to pray another prayer for your spouse based on Stormie Omartian's *Power of a praying wife*. This is a prayer every woman or pastor's wife should pray:

> *Lord, I pray that you will strengthen my husband to resist any temptation that comes his way. Stamp it out of his mind before it reaches his heart or personal experience. Lead him not into temptation but deliver him from evils such as adultery, pornography, drugs, alcohol, food addiction, gambling and perversion. Remove temptation, especially in the area of (name a specific temptation). Make him strong where he is weak. Help him to rise above anything that erects itself as a stronghold in his life. May he say, I will set nothing wicked before my eye; I hate the work of those who fall away; it shall not cling to me (Psalm 101:3). Lord, You've said that whoever has not rule over his own spirit is like a city broken down, without walls (Proverbs 25:28). I pray that (husband's name) will not be broken down by the power of evil, but raised up by the power of God. Establish a wall of protection around him. Fill him with your Spirit and flush out all that is not of You. Help him to take charge over his own spirit and have self-control to resist anything and anyone who becomes a lure. May he abhor what is evil and cling to what is good (Romans 12:9). I pray that he will be repulsed by tempting situations. Give him courage to reject them. Teach him to walk in the Spirit so he will not fulfill the lusts of the flesh.[20]*

THE CHARACTER OF
THE PASTOR'S WIFE

A few years ago, on a cold and dark winter's night, I stood by the window in my living room watching the snow reshape the ground outside. My husband was away at a retreat. The weather man predicted over twenty inches of snow. My heart was getting heavier in my chest as the night wore on. Many questions popped into my mind:

Is he going to get home safely?

What about the other folks on the trip, will they make it home to their families? I started praying for the Lord to clear away the snow so that everyone on the retreat would get home safely." Please Lord," I prayed, "Bring them home safely."

Patience is the fruit of the Spirit born into the heart and life of those whose roots are deep in the soil of God's love and grace. This fruit of patience is needed by every follower of Jesus Christ. This fruit of the Spirit is also needed in the life of those who serve the church. The bible depicts patience as part of the Christian's dress code: *Put on then, as God's chosen ones, holy and beloved, compassionate hearts, kindness, humility, meekness, and patience* (Colossians 3:12). Patience is often nurtured through trials. This is what Paul talks about when he said, "Not only that, but we rejoice in our sufferings, knowing that suffering produces endurance (or patience), and endurance produces character, and character produces hope, and hope does not put us to shame, because God's love has been poured into our hearts through the Holy Spirit who has been given to us. (Romans 5:3-5 ESV)

Leonardo da Vinci, the great Italian artist and sculptor said, "Patience serves as a protection against wrongs as clothes do against cold. For if you put on more clothes as the cold increases, it will have no power to hurt you. So in like manner you must grow in patience when you meet with great wrongs, and they will then be powerless to vex your mind."

Serving as a pastor's wife would be impossible without the Holy Spirit giving me the faith to endure and wait patiently for his perfect timing in my life, in the church and in our troubles. I have found that in the crucible of hardships or waiting on God for answered prayers, most pastors' wives have learned to develop this fruit in their lives. Without the fruit of patience I would not be able to tolerate the difficulties of being in a church where the demands on our family and my husband are high.

The pastor's wife has to be a source of encouragement to her husband, especially when they are contemplating a new ministry assignment. One day, as I was waiting before the Lord, I asked him, Lord what are you going to do within the life of this church? The pastor has touched the lives of so many people and it is difficult for them to see their spiritual leader depart for another congregation. This is very painful to watch the ripple of emotions affecting the families of the church. Thankfully, even though it is difficult to leave, churches do go on because it is God's church and God's people. Christ is the foundation not man. My husband often said "If a church falls apart when the pastor leaves one has to question if the foundation of that church was centered on the pastor instead of Christ." He is always mindful of this concern. Instead of hastily dispatching with these messy emotions, the pastor and family have to be patient with themselves and the congregation during these difficult transitions.

The other challenge and a place where we have to be patient is leaving ourselves open to taking new people into our lives. It is hard to give yourself to individuals in the church but you have to leave yourself open to God and learn to love them as brothers and sisters in the family of God. I believe that God uses people and situations in ministry to teach us and test us. God uses people and situations to remove dross from our lives and bring out pure gold or godly character. So we have to be patient in the midst of our trials. As the pastor's wife, I have committed myself to seek first Jesus and his kingdom (Matthew 6:33), and as a result I have seen all kinds of blessings flow into our daily lives.

Patience is vital. Every day I will tell myself, "Choose to rejoice today." No matter what the problem is, choose to rejoice. He holds my future in his hands. He holds my husband and my children in his hands. So then why worry, why fret? We are called to "Rejoice in hope, be patient in tribulation, be constant in prayer." (Romans 12: 12) The Lord is ruler and king over all aspects of our lives. I remind myself as much as I can that nothing can happen to me today, good or bad that has not already passed through his hands. So we do what James admonishes, "Be patient, therefore, brothers and sisters until the coming of the Lord. See how the farmer waits for the precious fruit of the earth, being patient about it, until it receives the early and the late rains." Like the farmer, we cannot make things grow or change. We are completely dependent on the Lord's will for our lives.

We learn as pastors' wives to trust our instincts. If we believe that our husbands are working too hard, or if they are stressed, we gently, and when necessary, firmly encourage them to slow down. As Paul told the Corinthians, "it is God who makes things grow (I Corinthians 3:7)," not the pastor!

CHERISH THE WORD

A s the pastor's wife, the word of God has to be your number one or principal resource for wisdom and courage for daily living. For me to go on from day to day with strength and joy, I turn to God's word daily for sustenance, encouragement, rebuke and direction. Just as prayer is my time to commune with God daily, constant intake of God's word is my opportunity to be quiet and listen to the Lord Jesus in response to the prayers I have prayed. By reading and meditating on God's word I find nothing is too hard for God. Our Lord is a promise keeper. All his promises are true and God will never violate his promises. This is why the Psalmist says,

> "In God, whose word I praise, in God I trust; I shall not be
> afraid. What can flesh do to me? Psalm 56: 4

God's word gives me wisdom and in the strength of this wisdom, I have parented our children, imparting to them and for the development of their faith, a love for God's word. As my children headed out the door for school each morning, I often sat at the table over breakfast and with them shared portions of Scripture. I wanted to feed them physical and spiritual food. Jesus wisely said, Man shall not live by bread alone but by every word that comes from the mouth of God (Matthew 4:4).

We wanted as a family to not just read and know Scripture in a robotic fashion; we wanted to know God through Scripture. Therefore the word of God had to be an integral part of our daily living. Moses' sense of the proximity of God's word and the people's ability to obey must not be missed. "But the word is very near you. It is in your mouth and in your heart, *so that you can do it* (Deuteronomy 30:14)."

There are days of deep disappointment. God's people can be hard, critical, and sweet all at the same time. Some days I hurt because of people's behavior. I live some days on the doorsteps of anger and bitterness. The door is wide open and I am beckoned to enter the house of anger, or find a room in the house of bitterness. Some days I just want to quit and encourage my family to move to another place, find another way of life and leave the world of the church behind. Without God's word I am certain I would have moved into one of those dark rooms and stayed there. By the grace of God, even though I stand at the door and everything in me says, "Go on in for a while;" I eventually walk away and find other ways to process my emotional pain.

Over the course of my life in the church as a pastor's wife, I have met burned out pastor's families. I have met pastors' wives who are bitter, cynical, and cold and who distance themselves from the people of the church. I have even met pastors' wives who stopped going to church as a way to cope and deal with their pain. I have walked in their shoes and I fully understand how those emotions can fill a person's heart. This is why Scripture has to be the number one resource to the pastor and his wife. The benefits of knowing and meditating on God's word are incalculable:

- **Keeps us from sin**: I have stored up your word in my heart that I might not sin against you. Psalm 119:11; I hold back my feet from every evil way, in order to keep your word (Psalm 119: 101).

- **Sustains us in trials:** Every word of God proves true; he is a shield to those who take refuge in him (Proverbs 30:5).

- **Provides wisdom and direction:** Your word is a lamp to my feet and a light to my pathway (Psalm 119: 105).

- **Fills us with joy:** Anxiety in a man's heart weighs him down, but a good word makes him glad (Proverbs 12:25).[21]

- **A spiritual weapon against the enemy:** Ephesians 6:17 talks about the word of God as a sword. Every Christian is called to take up this sword as a weapon used to resist the lies and distortions of Satan.[22]

- **Assures us of our salvation:** First, John explains, "But whoever keeps his word, in him truly the love of God is perfected. By this we may know that we are in him (I John 2:5)." An equally important assurance comes from I Peter 1:23: "Since you have been born again, not of perishable seed but of imperishable, through the living and abiding word of God"

I hope you get the picture. God's word is vital to our physical, spiritual and emotional health. The pastor must never use Scripture as a sermon mill for Sundays and ignore it the rest of the week. Like the deer panting for the water brook, even so must we desire God's word to satisfy our every thirst. So stay in the word of God so as to be filled with the words of God. It will cause you to speak life into your husband's ministry, and into your family's daily living. Even when the storm is raging remember Jesus wants us to trust him and to seek his peace. Satan has no desire to see the church prosper and grow in God's word. Satan hates it when people's lives are transformed through the word of God. I admonish you to cleave to the word of God; memorize it; live in obedience to God's word; order your life, your steps and your family according the promises and precepts of God's word. Remember what the Lord told Joshua as he was about to start his ministry:

> Only be strong and very courageous, being careful to do according to all the law that Moses my servant commanded you. Do not turn from it to the right hand or to the left, that you may have good success wherever you go. This Book of the Law (or word of God) shall not depart from your mouth, but you shall meditate on it day and night, so that you may be careful to do according to all that is written in it. For then you will make your way prosperous, and then you will have good success (Joshua 1:7-8 ESV).

FAITH SUSTAINING PRACTICES

I n his helpful book, *Celebration of Discipline,* Richard Foster wrote these true words, "Superficiality is the curse of our age . . . . The desperate need today is not for a greater number of intelligent people, or gifted people, but for deep people."[23]

Throughout my journey with Christ I have wanted to live a deep life of love for God and others. Here are some of the practices that have given order, direction and depth to my walk with God. I share these with you in the hope that you might be inspired to develop your own spiritual practices.

1. **Daily morning prayers** where I meet with God alone for meditation, solitude and waiting on God for his wisdom to fill my life.

2. **Daily prayer** time with my husband for our marriage, our children, our extended family and their salvation, for our finances, for our neighbors, people at the church, the health and spiritual well-being of the entire congregation, its leaders and all the families of the church, and prayers for current issues and hot spots in the world. In order to do this well we rise early each day to meet with God.

3. **Fasting with Prayer**: At least once per week I try to set aside a Wednesday or Thursday to fast and pray. What is

fasting for? Richard Foster gives a very helpful reminder to those who practice the discipline of fasting:

> The primary purpose of this practice is for focusing on God. Early on in this practice, the pangs of hunger may serve as reminders to focus our hearts on God. As we develop in this practice, fasting will result in an increasing spiritual sensitivity.[24]

We will be more "tuned in" to the Spirit's leading. We will be more aware of our own inner condition. We will be more aware of the needs of others. When Jesus was fasting in the desert he was tempted to turn stones into loaves of bread, but he said, "Man does not live on bread alone, but on every word that comes from the mouth of God" (Matthew 4:4). Another time, Jesus' disciples urged Jesus to eat some food (here, Jesus was not said to be fasting), he responded, "I have food to eat that you know nothing about . . . My food is to do the will of him who sent me and to finish the work" (John 4:32, 34). In abstaining from food and or drink, we discover an alternative source of strength.

If you recall, one reason for practicing spiritual disciplines is to eliminate the things that keep us from experiencing the fullness of life in God. Through this practice of abstaining from food and or drink, God can break our bondage to satisfying ourselves. Fasting reveals the things that control us.[25]

4. **Journal writing**: I keep a daily record of my prayers, Scriptures that speak to my life, events that unfold, my fears, my joys, and answers to prayers, disappointments and failures.

5. **Tithing**. This is also a spiritual discipline. Our family practices regular patterns of giving our money to the congregation. We do this to model what all leaders must do, but we primarily give out of obedience to God's word and love for God's work in the church and in the world. Along with regular tithing, we also practice generosity. This means we not only give money to those in need, we also try to be generous with our time, our material assets as a way to live out the admonitions of Scripture:

> What good is it, my brothers and sisters, if someone says he has faith but does not have works? Can that faith save him? If a brother or sister is poorly clothed and lacking in daily food, and one of you says to them, "Go in peace, be warmed and filled," without giving them the things needed for the body, what good is that? So also faith by itself, if it does not have works, is dead (James 2:14-17 ESV).

6. **Hospitality**: Scripture reminds us to do this: "Contribute to the needs of the saints and seek to show hospitality (Romans 12:13)." Furthermore, "Show hospitality to one another without grumbling (I Peter 4:9)." Throughout our ministry we have used our home as a place of ministry. I am not suggesting this is for everyone, but one of my

delights of ministry in the church is the chance to show hospitality to people. Each Christmas or Thanksgiving we look for a family, student, widow, someone who needs a friend, and we invite them to have dinner with us. Throughout the year we try to systematically invite our neighbors and people from the church to spend time in our home. This is not a time to prepare a four-course gourmet meal. We invite people over for pizza, dessert and coffee, or sometimes a Jamaican meal, complete with Curried chicken, or Jerk chicken.

7. **Evangelism**: God has done so many wonderful things in my life and I try to find ways to share Christ with people in the church, places I have worked, my neighborhood and with strangers I meet. I love Matthew's depiction of Jesus:

> When he saw the crowds, he had compassion for them, because they were harassed and helpless, like sheep without a shepherd (Matthew 9:36).

God has called us to be a witness to the resurrection of Jesus to a dying world. I take to heart these words: For I am not ashamed of the gospel, for it is the power of God for salvation to everyone who believes, to the Jew first and also to the Greek (Romans 1:16 ESV).

Amazingly, God has used my feeble attempts to introduce people to Jesus and many of them are still walking with the Lord today!

Let me issue a word of caution here: even though I do these things, I am not trying to earn my salvation. God does not love me more because I practice these disciplines. I am still a sinner saved by grace; I still struggle with my fears and moments of self-doubt. I practice these disciplines in light of what Paul says: But I discipline my body and keep it under control, lest after preaching to others I myself should be disqualified (1 Corinthians 9:27 ESV).

CONCLUSION

Finishing well

The joys and the agonies of ministry are inseparable. There is no way to have one without the other. During the hard times we think the hard times will never end. As my mother always said, "This too will pass." Do not let the challenges in ministry eviscerate the joys, and there are many great joys. For example, I remember when our children were young and we took the church's youth group to an amusement park. I was pregnant at the time so I could not go on the rides. My husband did not like to ride roller coasters so he stayed with me and we did not get to ride but the kids in the youth group had so much fun. While they were on the roller coasters they would call out to us as they screamed with excitement. We forged an important bond with these teens, but we also created an unforgettable memory that we will take to the grave.

Like Paul, I am learning to find contentment in whatever state I am in (Philippians 4:11). I have learned to appreciate abundance, but I am also learning that all my needs and concerns not met in my time will always be met in God's time. Through it all I have seen the faithfulness of God. By faith I believe that all I have been through is somehow being used by God to the praise and the glory of his name.

With God's strength and the doors He chooses to open I intend to share some of my life lessons with other pastors' wives. It is a great thing to be a help meet to a man of God called to the ministry. You are part of a wonderful calling. See yourself as called to be a pastor's wife, and take it seriously. The quality and integrity of the ministry will be shaped by your support or lack of support for the work God has placed in your hand.

Today, I am at a different point in my life. I am learning to let go of the past and to press ahead. I do not know what the future holds but I know who holds my future. I also know that I want to finish the race God has put before me with joy. I want to finish well. Keep spending time in prayer especially if you are a young minister's wife. Develop your relationship with the Lord; may it grow deep and strong. When all is said and done, the greatest thing we can do is to love the Lord God with our entire being. This is what Jesus said, "You shall love the Lord your God with all your heart and with all your soul and with all your mind. This is the great and first commandment. And a second is like it: You shall love your neighbor as yourself (Matthew 22:38-39 ESV)."

Even if you get no earthly reward the Lord will reward you. Your children and your husband will call you blessed. It is a unique and wonderful call to be a pastor's wife. The joy of the Lord continues to be my strength. I do not fear when the heat comes because I am planted by life giving rivers of water. Jesus wants me to bear good fruit that will last forever. I pray I have touched somebody and my living has not been in vain.

Finally, in order to finish well we must have a vision that looks beyond the present. Without a vision life becomes mired in small, inconsequential matters. Your vision is not to have the biggest church, or to live in an upper class neighborhood—that is too small. Your vision should be to use every ounce of your life to do what Micah demands:

> "He has told you, O man, what is good;
> and what does the Lord require of you
> but to do justice, and to love kindness,
> and to walk humbly with your God? (Micah 6:8)

But I also want to finish well so that like Samuel, at the close of his ministry, I might be able to say with humility and great joy, "Behold, I have obeyed your voice in all that you have said to me and have made a king over you. And now, behold, the king walks before you, and I am old and gray; and behold, my sons are with you. I have walked before you from my youth until this day. Here I am; testify against me before the LORD and before his anointed. *Whose ox have I taken? Or whose donkey have I taken? Or whom have I defrauded? Whom have I oppressed? Or from whose hand have I taken a bribe to blind my eyes with it?* Testify against me and I will restore it to you. (1 Samuel 12:1-3 ESV)

Not too long ago, I called up a past member of a congregation we served to wish her happy birthday. She was overjoyed to hear from me and told me that my taking the time to call her on her birthday was just the best thing that happened to her that day. She kept saying how much she loved us and missed us, and that our call was the icing on the cake. Almost to tears, I could hear her voice crack with emotion over the phone and she again wanted me to know how much she missed us and loved us and how we had touched the lives of people.

Having the chance to look back on these years of ministry through the writing of this book has been most rewarding. It causes me to reflect on the things I would like to change about myself. Also, being able to reflect on my past journey affords me the opportunity, since I am still involved in ministry, to not take myself too seriously. It also makes me think about the legacy I will leave for the next generation of pastors' wives. I love to hear when people say, "We had a wonderful pastor's wife." In many cases, this is what is often said. The times I have been able to meet and talk with pastors' wives, I often hear how disillusioned they are with the ministry. Thankfully, I still hear about many cases where the pastor's wife loves the people and they are very grateful that the congregation treats their husband with respect. Many share how they have drawn closer to the Lord as a result of being a pastor's wife. On the other hand, some say they are glad they are no longer in the ministry because the responsibilities of the job are too stressful. So if you are planning to marry a minister, married to one, or engaged to one, I hope you have gleaned some insights from some of the experiences or what I have learned from others who have shared their experiences with me.

One day, the faithful pastor's wife will hear the Lord say:

Well done, good and faithful servant. You have been faithful over a little; I will set you over much. Enter into the joy of your master (Matthew 25:23). This is what I want us all to think about as we support our husbands in ministry. I know I have shared many verses of Scripture with you, but here's another gem from Psalm 105:4: "Seek the Lord and his strength, seek his presence continually." Our greatest delight is not found in the church, or in a spouse; our greatest delight is found in the Lord. The blessing that comes with seeking the Lord is the assurance that even as I walk through deep waters, the Lord wants me to know that he is in the midst of my challenges. Thank God that I am still involved in ministry.

Today I am a Marriage and Family Therapist, eagerly giving my time and energy to show others the way they must go in their marriages, in raising their children, but also trying to empower people who feel they cannot go on because of the pressures of this life. Serving as a Marriage and Family therapist is now an important part of what the Lord has shown me that he wants me to do at this point in my life. So as you walk the road of ministry as pastors' wives, remember, Christ is there all the time eagerly waiting to bless and provide all that you need to accomplish his will for your life. All things are possible for those who believe that God is able to do more than they could ever ask, think, or conceive.

On December 24, 1983 Ray and I walked out of our home congregation in Jamaica. We had just publically declared our vows before God, our family and friends to cherish and honor each other *till death do we part.* The theme song for our wedding printed on the bulletin said:

> *We've come this far by faith*
> *Leaning on the Lord*
> *Trusting in His holy word*
> *He's never failed me yet*[26]

Twenty nine years later, we are still singing this song in praise of God's faithfulness!

Soli Deo Gloria!

ENDNOTES

1   Eugene H. Peterson, The Pastor: A Memoir (New York, NY: Harper Collins, 2011), 95.

2   Bill Hybels, *Courageous Leadership* (Grand Rapids, Michigan: Zondervan, 2002), 12.

3   The Francis A Schaeffer Institute of Christian Leadership: Church Leadership.org. Article written by R. J. Krejcir Ph.D

4   Dorothy Kelley Patterson, *A Handbook for Ministers' Wives: Sharing the blessings of your marriage, family and home,* (Nashville, TN: B&H Publishing Group, 2002), 3.

5   Matilda E. Andross, *Alone with God: Fitting for Service,* (Mountain View, California: Pacific Press, 1917), 22

6   Ibid.

7   Frank Laubach, *Prayer: The Mightiest Force in the World* (Westwood, N.J.: F. H. Revell Co., 1946), 18.

8   Dorothy Kelley Patterson, *A Handbook for Ministers' Wives: Sharing the blessings of your marriage, family* (Nashville, TN: Broadman and Holman Publishers, 2002),1

9   http://www.buildingchurch.net/g2s-i.htm

10 Frances Havergal, *Like a River Glorious,* 1874

11 Wayne Cordiero, *Leading on Empty: Refilling Your Tank and Renewing Your Passion* (Minneapolis, MN: Bethany House Publishers, 2009), 13.

12 Ibid, 14-16

13 Visit http://www.familylife.com/events/featured-events/week end-to-remember for more information and details about this event

[14] Ministry is always exciting as you see how God is working to provide, change, and lead. However it can also be a real drain on your relationship with your spouse with long hours, extra meetings, counseling, and being on call 24/7 for your congregation. How do you get refreshment and help for YOUR marriage? At FamilyLife we understand your struggles and that is why we offer half-price discounts or a registration scholarship for all senior pastor couples or full-time associate pastor couples. (This is the quote on their website)

[15] Stormie Omartian, *The Power of a praying wife* (Eugene, Oregon: Harvest House Publishers, 1997), 129

[16] Ibid, 76

[17] Stanley J. Grenz; Roy D. Bell, *Betrayal of Trust: Confronting and Preventing Clergy Sexual Misconduct*, (Grand Rapids, MI: Baker Book Group, 2001), 10

[18] Ibid, 8

[19] Gary D. Chapman, *The five love languages: the secret to love that lasts* (Chicago, IL: Northfield publishing: 2010), 14

[20] Omartian, 77-78

[21] This good word may come through others, but here the good word that gladdens an anxious heart is Scripture.

[22] Also see Revelation 12:11: here the word of God is relied upon to defeat the lies and accusations of Satan against God's righteous ones: *And they have conquered him by the blood of the Lamb and by the word of their testimony, for they loved not their lives even unto death.*

[23] Richard J. Foster, *The Celebration of discipline: the path of spiritual growth* (San Francisco: HarperCollins, 1988), 1

[24] Ibid, 67

[25] Ibid, 48

[26] Albert A. Goodson, author (1963)

BIBLIOGRAPHY

Andross, Matilda E. Alone with God: Fitting for Service. Mountain View: CA Pacific Press, 1917.

Chapman, Gary D. The five love languages: the secret to love that lasts. Chicago, IL: Northfield publishing, 2010.

Cordiero, Wayne. Leading on Empty: Refilling Your Tank and Renewing Your Passion. (Minneapolis, MN: Bethany House Publishers, 2009.

Foster, Richard J. The Celebration of discipline: the path of spiritual growth. San Francisco: HarperCollins, 1988.

Goodson, Albert A. We've come this far by faith. 1963.

Grenz, Stanley J., and Roy D. Bell. Betrayal of Trust: Confronting and Preventing Clergy Sexual Misconduct. Grand Rapids, MI: Baker Book Group, 2001.

Havergal, Frances. Like a River Glorious. 1874.

Hybels, Bill. Courageous Leadership. Grand Rapids: Zondervan, 2002.

Krejcir, Dr. Richard J. "Church Leadership.org." Churchleadership. org. 2007. http://www.churchleadership.org/apps/articles/default.asp?articleid=42347&columnid=4545&contentonly=true (accessed April 24, 2012).

Laubach, Frank. Prayer: The Mightiest Force in the World. Westwood, N.J: F. H. Revell Co, 1946.

Omartian, Stormie. The Power of a praying wife. Eugene, Oregon: Harvest House Publishers, 1997.

Patterson, Dorothy Kelley. A Handbook for Ministers' Wives: Sharing the blessings of your marriage, family and home. Nashville: B&H Publishing Group, 2002.

Made in the USA
Lexington, KY
04 February 2019